MW00942589

TRUTHS FOR OUR HEARTS

Lights Shining in a Dark Place

Donald R. Latimer

WestBow Press books may be ordered through booksellers or by contacting:

WestBow Press
A Division of Thomas Nelson & Zondervan
1663 Liberty Drive
Bloomington, IN 47403
www.westbowpress.com
1 (866) 928-1240

ISBN: 978-1-9736-0886-8 (sc)
ISBN: 978-1-9736-0887-5 (hc)
ISBN: 978-1-9736-0885-1 (e)

Library of Congress Control Number: 2017918063

Print information available on the last page.

WestBow Press rev. date: 12/18/2017

Contents

INTRODUCTION

In early 2010 something happened for me in my walk of faith that I want to share with other believers. I found a path to a new depth for my faith that I didn't know could exist. It is my sincere hope that I can help others understand how to find this same path. I now realize there is a special place of fellowship that almost seems to lie secret and hidden within our own faith, but there is a way for all of us to be inspired to trust God that could and should radically change our lives. We can walk more surrendered in our faith and less entangled in all the cares of this world if we can learn to embrace our faith consciously and intentionally with everything that is in us so that through that faith we might find the true sweetness of a fellowship with Jesus that only a surrendered heart can know.

I feel compelled to give witness of what I have found, having wanted and sought after a deeper relationship with my Lord for almost thirty years. Yet, a true depth of faith seemed hidden from me, as if a veil covered my eyes and kept me from finding that faith, but now something has happened for me that has caused me to feel like I see past the veil. I am excited at what I have found and I hope to encourage all believers to a more sincere, more genuine, more surrendered, more passionate and powerful way of walking out our lives led by our King who reigns from on high, Jesus our Christ.

I am convinced that knowing these few truths that I want to share could change anyone's life forever. I know that just the knowledge of them alone is not where the true value is, but the working out of them in our lives is what could change us. I hope you will listen with an open heart and examine carefully to see if what I'm sharing touches your heart as truth. I know that if anyone is affected in such a way so as to open the eyes of their hearts to see deeper into the depths and the riches of what God has done for us, it will be worth all the effort I can give it.

Because of my own experience, I have come to realize that wc believers often don't comprehend how precious to God is a life truly lived through Jesus, a life that has found that genuine sanctified walk. It proves to all those around us, really to all the world, that through His death and life we can be set free from the bondage and entanglements of this world in such a way that we are able to live a life pleasing to God.

Here is a list of truths I will be focusing on in more detail chapter by chapter.

1) The hardness of our hearts, even as believers, can be hidden from us.
2) The motives behind why we do the things we do can be hidden from our awareness by our hearts deceitfulness.
3) We don't necessarily walk a life pleasing to God just because we have believed in Jesus.
4) It is not just the action that we do that matters, but it is the thoughts and intents of our hearts that lay behind those actions that really matters.

5) We can try to see how we are on our own, but because of how deceptive our hearts are, we need Jesus to guide our every step.
6) Jesus has made a way to guide us, through His Spirit He has put within us, that will lead us correctly in love every time.
7) We can be led by His Spirit in how to respond to all that goes on in our heart, both how to deal with our thoughts themselves, and how to respond in love to those around us.
8) We need to act on His guidance not just know it. Learning His truths is of little value if we don't apply them through faith into how we walk in love.
9) We can only produce fruit if we walk a life led by His Spirit.
10) God is involved and in control of all that happens around us. He is in control of all the testing and trials that take place in our lives.
11) Access to a walk led by His Spirit is equally available to all believers.
12) It is entering this walk of obedience to the leading of His Spirit through faith that will truly make us different from all other people.

As I explain my thoughts about these truths, I am going to include some of the story about how my heart was opened to see them. Perhaps some of the questions that took place in my heart and things that triggered them will touch something inside your heart as well.

I can say with all certainty that if you knew what this walk I am sharing about was really like, you would want it. If I could help you to see what I have seen. If I could explain its value to you, you would give all you have to get it. For me, it truly has turned out to be ***"the pearl of great price."***

I want to extend a special note of thanks and acknowledgement to my wife Michelle for her time and effort in reading and rereading my writing and to my sisters Karen and Jeannie.

Thanks you guys for your help, your support and your encouragement.

Donald R. Latimer

For anyone wanting to contact me, you can email me at:

don@truthsforourhearts.com

Chapter 1

MY YEARS TRYING TO BE A GOOD CHRISTIAN

In 1980 I got saved, Christian speak, meaning I came to a place where I believed in my heart in what God said: I was a sinner; God sent Jesus, His Son, to be my savior; Jesus died on a cross paying for my sin; and by believing in Him, I was saved from God's judgment. I could go on with a bit more theology, but the truth is, I can't tell you how much I knew beyond these very basic truths. But something within me was bearing witness to me that I was saved. I don't think my actual experience of salvation is even fully explainable. It was an act of faith accompanied by a sense of assurance. I had believed God and something special had happened.

At the time, I suppose that was all I really knew. In the months following, I was sometimes driven, but at the very least always drawn to want to know more, to want to understand more. I read the Bible through, cover to cover, as quickly as I could. I reasoned that if I believed God spoke to us through this book, I was excited to find out what He said. I quickly discovered that I didn't really understand all I was reading. I pressed on to get what I could on my own, and at the same time sought out other Christians to help explain things to me. I came to realize that we were all trying to understand the mysteries of God together. We all seemed to possess the same assurance of faith, but understanding all the things about God through the teachings of the Bible was a little more elusive. Nonetheless, I sought out Christian friends to fellowship with and continued to try to understand the mysteries of my new faith, both from my own studies and through the teachings of other Christians.

Within the first few months, I sought out a mature Christian teacher, and asked him to mentor me by going through the Bible, book by book, or sometimes, verse by verse, and answering questions for me. Much of this I did with him one on one, on a more personal level than I could get anywhere else. To this day I am thankful for the methodology he taught me to use in studying the Bible. I also used books, radio teachings, pastors and teachers at church and elsewhere, artists in their music, and Christian friends, all in the hope of growing myself as a mature Christian. At the time I thought of myself as the typical Christian who was very serious about their faith.

The months of being a new believer quickly turned into years and before I knew it, more than 28 years had passed. I pause at this point in time in order to give an assessment of where I think my heart was in my walk with the Lord. I knew who Jesus was and still believed in Him, but my religion itself had become of less importance in my life. I was around non-believers more than believers, although I did try to share with them how to be saved by believing in Jesus when I thought it appropriate. I think my sharing sounded out to them more like just so much theology. I had knowledge of the truth, but I lacked the passion that can come from a sincere faith. Other than knowing that I had escaped judgment from hell, my faith had not done all that much to benefit and change how I really was inside. I don't want you to misunderstand, my faith was precious to me and I felt committed in my heart to never deny Jesus my Lord. The assurance from within had never left me; I knew I had believed in Jesus and that I was saved. But I suppose, I was not very happy about where my life was headed. I was a bit disillusioned about my religion and I really didn't make much place for it in my life anymore.

Times leading up to my change

In 2008, my daughter came to me and asked me what I thought about some Bible prophesies she was studying. The exact verses she questioned me about don't matter that much, but somehow her questions birthed in me a desire for a little study of my own on the prophesies in the Bible. I know there is probably no area for Christians where understanding the mysteries, of what God has said in the Bible, seems more hidden and elusive than in prophesies. So, I want to assure you up front, right now, that I am not going to try to share about what I think is coming prophetically other than is necessary to explain my story.

In the beginning, I think the main question I was looking to answer for myself was could I get a fix on where we were, prophetically speaking, on God's time line. I thought I was pretty aware of much of the better known teachings on the subject, so to make this study different for me, I really wanted to be committed to just reading the scriptures themselves and sticking to a firsthand look, so to speak. I reasoned that I could be sure the scriptures themselves were true, and I didn't want to be influenced in what I thought they might be saying from outside input or having my thinking and my approach to understanding them contaminated by the approach of someone else.

In a short time, I was off poring through the prophesies on my own. I often read for hours on end. Over the next year and a half, I became more and more obsessed with my studies. I didn't keep track, but a guess is I was averaging a few hours a day, from one end of the Bible to the other, looking for clues in anything God might have said. I was reading the prophetic areas over and over, but I wasn't leaving other areas out. A note of interest that was happening for me, is that the more I studied the Bible, the more I was convinced it had the answers; it was all perfectly true and if God would just open my understanding so I could get it, it would make perfect sense. I was more and more sure it wasn't missing any information; I was just blinded in my understanding. I was aware at the time that I was trying to understand the greatest, and yet maybe the most obscure, mystery of all time. I love a mystery and I was both passionate and excited by this one. What seemed to entice me on and fuel my passion to study was believing I was making progress in my understanding.

What happened to me next is really the most important point of interest in this whole story. I had been doing my little obsessed study for a little over a year when I began to question myself about my own heart. If you have read through what most consider the Old Testament prophesies, one can't help but see how God hammers Israel for having a hard heart toward Him. Over and over He describes them as a stiff necked, hard hearted, obstinate and rebellious people. In fact, this seems to be why He is so compelled to judge them. But as I studied this over and over, I began to ask myself a perplexing question. How can this people, of all the people throughout time, be so blind? For forty years they see God's hand in their lives every single day, in ways we only wish we could see once in a lifetime. If you believe in the literal plagues that took place at Moses hand, then think about all that happened before their eyes to get them out of Egypt. Then look at all that took place over the next forty years: water from the rock, manna from heaven daily for the entire time, pillar of fire to lead them by night, a cloud to lead them by day, their shoes and their clothing not wearing out for forty years, the earth opening up to swallow Korah and his group and you get the picture.

I don't think there is really any way for us to begin to comprehend how this group of chosen people felt about themselves or how they actually felt toward God. Think about all that they saw for a moment. There has never been a group of people who have seen more of the wonders of God first hand than this group that came out of Egypt. The expectation, of course, is that they of all people would be the most committed to follow God in any and every way possible. So why does it seem to appear from God's perspective that the opposite is true? How come they couldn't see how hard they were toward God's ways? The mystery is how they could have witnessed all that they saw for all those years, and how strong you would think this should have made their faith in their God, and yet it didn't seem to. For me, the answer to all their disobedience did not seem to get clearer the more I studied, in fact, the opposite happened. The more I understood about all the miracles God did bringing Israel out of Egypt and during those forty years that followed, the less how they acted toward God as a people made sense to me. But then I started to ask myself an interesting question. If this group of God's chosen people could be so blind with all they had seen, what about me? Was it possible I could have a hard heart and not know it?

As I continued my studies focused on all the prophetic scriptures where God pounds on about their hard heart, the questioning within me about my own heart and whether or not it could be hard grew. In the beginning, I tried to sluff the whole idea off. I thought of myself as a pretty reasonable guy. I was pretty good to the people I worked with, to my friends, to my kids, even to my ex-wife. If I was hard hearted, I was not seeing it. I thought of myself as a pretty loving and caring person. Yet the questions lingered and grew and as I continued to look at myself. I wondered all the more, was I really being honest? As I think back, this questioning look at my own heart went on for many weeks,maybe even months, and a sort of honesty began to brew in the background. Glimpses of times I thought maybe I hardened my heart a little, with this or that decision, started to surface. I began to see things I had done in my past, even as a saved dedicated believer, when if honest, I had to admit I did not act in love the way Jesus would have acted.

I thought about my own divorce. If I had been a genuinely mature Christian in my faith, what would have, or should have, been my reaction to the trials that God had allowed to happen in my marriage? Had I loved my wife with the love of Christ? As my studies of God pounding on Israel for their hard heart went on, keep in mind I was logging often hours a day listening to God chastise this chosen people. The questions continued to brew in my heart and I wondered all the more about my own honesty. Thoughts about things I had done, even at the peaks of my most committed walk with the Lord, continued to surface. Now the question that I started to ask myself was, "Had I ever really loved my wife or anyone for that matter in the sacrificial way that the scriptures taught?" If I saw myself as such a committed Christian, why was I now seeing that for all my commitment, I still hadn't loved unselfishly? Had I loved to be loved? And when I didn't get all I wanted, then had I withheld my love? Was my heart ever even fully given to love my wife as I should have in the first place?

The more honest I got with myself about all this, the more I began to see and question my own failings. I knew if I were to argue and present my case of how I had acted and walked my life before men, by the way we judge, nobody was going to find me guilty. Throughout this time of questioning myself, as I talked with my friends and family about the possibility of me having a hard heart no one was telling me they thought that about me. They didn't see me as being a hard person. Everyone seemed to think I was a pretty nice guy. But the question going on inside me was, "If I hadn't loved sacrificially the way Jesus taught, and I knew that I hadn't, what kind of love was that?" "Would I really be divorced if I had been obedient to what Jesus taught about how to love?"

However wrong I might have thought my ex-wife was, in my case I was pretty sure, if I would have loved her even just from the beginning of our Christian walk, the way I should have, we would not have ended up divorced. It was as if God was opening my heart and eyes to see myself, to see how hard my heart had been. It wasn't just that I had been hard toward my wife, which I could now see I had, but it was that I had been hard toward God in that I had not loved the way He had wanted me too. The more I looked at myself, the more little decisions came to my mind. Decision after decision where I had not loved the way I could have, or should have; where I had not done the things God would have wanted me to do.

As I thought about the way I had walked my faith, or should I really say, the way I had failed to walk my faith, I started to become horrified by the thoughts of the influences it may have had on my kids, on my grand-kids, my friends and the world around me. What had my kind of a Christian walk said about what I thought was OK? My eyes were opening up to see how I was not walking a Christian faith, but a life with an obstinate and hard heart just like Israel. Through my divorce and the path I had chosen, God had allowed my sin to become magnified to the point where even my hard heart could now see it. What was I to do? I want to make something clear here. You may be thinking I'm talking about seeing how messed up I was at the peak of some back slide in life, but the truth is I was more focused about looking at the times when I thought of myself as the most committed Christian I had ever been. I knew that even at the peak of my commitment to the Lord, I had not walked in the love of Christ the way I knew I should have.

As I sit here, even years later, I know I can't go back and fix the influences that took place as a result of how I was failing to walk out my faith because of such a hard heart. The most I can do to make up for my failings is get it right from here forward.

In asking the question, how could Israel be so blind, or the more enlightened question, how could I be so blind, as to have such a hard heart? Moses in these next verses sheds a little light on the answer for me and I hope for all of us.

> *Deut 29:2 -5 And Moses summoned all Israel and said to them, "You have seen all that the LORD did before your eyes in the land of Egypt to Pharaoh and all his servants and all his land; the great trials which your eyes have seen, those great signs and wonders. "Yet to this day the LORD has not given you a heart to know, nor eyes to see, nor ears to hear. "I have led you forty years in the wilderness; your clothes have not worn out on you, and your sandal has not worn out on your foot.*

As it turns out, the problem Israel had was the same problem I had, God had not given me a heart to know or eyes to see.

I think of myself as a pretty typical Christian. I'm probably not really much different than any other believer reading this right now, so I hope you will join me in this next question. Are any of us really capable of being honest with ourselves, about how we are in our hearts? Maybe like Israel, we just won't see how hard our hearts are if God doesn't give us a heart to know. If God does not open our hearts to see how messed up we are, maybe we just are not going to see it.

The hardness of our hearts can be hidden from us

Now I want to pause my story for a bit and focus on the first truth I want to try to share with anyone who can receive it. We, even as believers, can have hard hearts. I have become convinced that, almost universally, we are blind to this condition. If God does not open our eyes we cannot see, and if we think we see without Him, we end up being all the more blind. I think one of the things that keeps us so blind to God's truths is this pride in thinking we already know. I know of nothing more crippling to my walk than this struggle with my proud heart. Now the question I had asked about Israel, "How blind could they be, to be so obstinate and hard hearted," was being turned back on me and it is really something all of us as Christians have to reckon with. Does this, a second group of God's chosen people, us, have hard hearts just like the first?

In this verse from Jeremiah, God gives us some insight into both the source of the problem, and if we care to look closely, I believe the extent of it.

> ***Jer 17:9 "The heart is more deceitful than all else And is desperately sick; Who can understand it?***

The interesting thing about this assessment in Jeremiah is that it isn't necessarily about Israel; it is just an open ended assessment of man's heart. I am convinced it is just as accurate of an assessment of my heart as a believer, of all of our hearts as believers, as it ever was about Israel.

I started this writing by stating, "I believe I have discovered truths about my Christian walk that are so important, extraordinary and amazing that I want to share them with other believers." So here is the second part to this first major truth I want to share with you. I want to state it as clearly and as plainly as I possibly can. We, all of us as Christians, because of our hard hearts are a group of messed up believers. First, we are messed up because we can't see we are messed up. Maybe you are saying in your heart, "You might be messed up but not me." I want to share what I have come to see as the only enlightened position on this truth. If you see that you are messed up, but understand that you actually are not capable of comprehending the depths of the problem on your own, if you have come to the conclusion that you can only really see the errors of your ways when God reveals them to you, if you truly believe this in your heart, not just in your theology, than you have actually understood a truth. As long as you think in your heart you are capable of seeing where you are messed up on your own, with your own mind, you are blind to this truth. Here are some verses from 1st John I want to share, but I would like you to read the same verses with the thought of ***messed up*** substituted for the word ***sin***. I believe my re-write captures the essence of the truth John hoped to communicate with his reader and I think this is pretty OK to do because if we walk in sin, that is pretty messed up.

> *1 John 1:8-10 If we say that we have no sin, we are deceiving ourselves and the truth is not in us. If we confess our sins, He is faithful and righteous to forgive us our sins and to cleanse us from all unrighteousness. If we say that we have not sinned, we make Him a liar and His word is not in us.*

Now, 1 John 1:8-10, with my re-write: If we say that we are not messed up, we are deceiving ourselves and the truth is not in us. But if we will confess we are messed up, He is faithful and righteous to forgive us for being messed up and to cleanse us from all unrighteousness. If we say that we are not messed up, we make Him a liar and His word is not in us.

The only way we are ever going to get our walk straightened out is when we realize that **it has to be by His power; His power first, for us to see the problems and second, His power for us to have victory over those problems. This is not a self help thesis. We cannot fix ourselves.** There is only one thing of value I can hope to accomplish with this writing and that is if I can help us to somehow be honest enough in our hearts so that we get to the point where we turn to Him and ask Him to open our eyes. We can do this today. We can do this right now, but no one can do this for us. It doesn't matter if we are the pastor of a mega-church with thousands of people following us or an eight year old child who just became a believer. We still need the Lord to show us and fix us or we will not become fixed. If we do not get the log out of our eyes on this one, so that we can see what our righteousness really looks like to a Holy God, we as a chosen people are going to remain of little or no help to those around us, including the ones we love the most.

Teaching and sharing all the theology and doctrines we can accumulate with those around us will never be a good substitute. But if we can see our true condition, if we can be honest in our hearts before God, if we can admit how messed up we are, how entangled and enslaved in all the course of this world we have become, how we have become caught up in the works of our hands, caught up in the desires of our eyes, loving the pleasures we seek, blind to the selfishness of our own hearts, then there will be hope for us.

going to remain of little or no help to those around us, including the ones we love the most.

Teaching and sharing all the theology and doctrines we can accumulate with those around us will never be a good [illegible] benefit. But if we can see our true condition, if we can be honest in our hearts before God, if we can admit how messed up we are, how entangled and enslaved in all the course of this world we have become, how we have become caught up in the words of our heads, caught up in the desires of our eyes, chasing the pleasures we seek, blind to the selfishness of our own hearts, then there will be hope for us.

Chapter 2

HOW WAS I GOING TO LIVE MY LIFE?

A couple of things happened for me as I looked at my life more honestly. My heart had been opened enough to understand that I was not truly living my life in a way that was pleasing to the Lord; I was beginning to see how focused and entangled I had become in the things of my little world; I was becoming aware of choices I was making everyday and of choices I had made in the past that were not the choices that Jesus would have wanted me to make. The second thing that was going on in my heart was a growing awareness that there was a relationship, a fellowship, a closeness in a way of walking with Jesus that I sensed was available for me, but I knew I didn't have yet. It seemed to be held off from me by a decision to surrender I needed to make. Did I really want all I could have in my walk with the Lord?

As I looked ahead at the whole idea of following Him in a truly honest and serious way that would be pleasing to Him, I was starting to realize that the desire to have this closeness with Jesus was going to be tied to the choices I was making throughout the day in the way I was living my life. I sensed it was wrapped up in a challenge to walk a life of faith filled with a sincere love guided by His teachings in the Bible. I wanted to be genuine in understanding what Jesus' kind of love would really look like. Not my idea of love, or the worlds idea of love, but a true selfless sacrificial love that would look like the way Jesus would want me to do things. If I was going to find the closeness with Him I desired for my life, I needed to find a way for my heart to be surrendered to His desires and I needed it to be both honest and real before Him.

As time passed, the challenge that was going on in my heart grew. Was I willing to surrender all to have a walk of faith with Jesus or not? I could see my heart weighing out what it might cost me to be surrendered. Was the loss of the pleasures of living my life to please myself in all the areas I could come up with going to be reason enough for me to give up on this desire to go after a close walk with Jesus? As I look back, I realize I was also looking at all the excuses that could be made to put this decision off or maybe find someway to find a bit of a compromise. I actually remember thinking about waiting a bit, I guess, so I could enjoy the pleasures of doing things my way for a little longer. After all, wouldn't Jesus let me start walking with Him whenever I decided I wanted to? I wondered, if I chose to delay, would I ever make the decision at all? I wanted to know what a fully committed walk with Jesus might be like and it seemed to me, deciding to delay my start, would undermine the depths of any relationship I could hope to have with Him. I knew that any intentional compromise was not really following what the Lord was challenging me to do.

The challenge seemed to be more about obedience. Was I going to come up with whatever excuses and do the stiff neck hard heart self centered approach I had unconsciously done in the past trying to deceive myself into believing that the way I was as a Christian was good enough and I didn't need to change or fix anything, or was I going to surrender my life, by trying to live it pleasing to Him, by obeying Him anywhere and everywhere with all I could understand or know He might want me to do?

I also thought about the justification of not focusing so much on what goes on in my heart, because we all sin, especially in our thought life and no one is expected to have a completely sinless life anyway, right? This seemed to be just another way I could harden my heart toward what He wanted me to do that was floating around in my thoughts. But I knew the question I was wrestling with was not, could I walk a sinless life or even how much victory following Jesus might produce, but did I care about what was going on in my heart and did I want to try to live my life to please Jesus? I think the challenge of the moment was, "Did I have enough faith to try to see where this would all go and just put all the excuses aside?"

Was I going to surrender to do whatever I believed Jesus wanted me to do with no consideration for what it might cost me, no compromising, total surrender? Could I stop being afraid of how He might allow me to be tested? Could I trust that He loves me no matter what the test might be or what would come? Could I get to the place where I just accepted that if I do things His way, it will always be the best way? At the time, I had a sense that this was a huge decision for me that would forever change my life. In the past, I had been pretty blind to all these conversations of my heart related to the decision of obedience I was facing now. I think they were always going on, I just didn't have eyes to see them. I believe that we make unconscious decisions all day long mostly unaware of all these conversations that are going on in the background of our hearts, unaware of the excuses we make and actually unaware of the real reasons behind why we do the things we do. Which is why I want anyone willing to hear it to consider this truth I'm sharing, **"That the motives behind why we do the things we do can be hidden from our awareness by our hearts deceitfulness."** I think we need to understand that the motives behind how we really walk, even as Christians, can be hidden from us by that deceitfulness, and it is something to be reckoned with by each one of us. If we deceive ourselves, as I did for thirty years, believing I was walking a life pleasing to God because I was a good Christian, but in truth I selfishly walked led by my own desires. Will there ever be any hope for us to see the truth? I think we have to begin to comprehend how our hearts really work. If our hearts are capable of deceiving us, then we need His help to see through that deceitfulness. Maybe you're a pastor or a dedicated missionary or someone who sees themselves as having served the Lord your entire life. That doesn't change the importance of understanding this truth because a lifetime of serving the Lord doesn't change the nature of our hearts. Our hearts are still capable of deceiving us about our true motives. I am convinced we can not see through to the truth of why we do the things we do without His help. Our walk is before a holy God who sees straight into our hearts. He knows our every thought and He knows the true motives behind all we do. He is the judge. If we are not walking our lives in love the way He wants us to, no matter what we tell ourselves, we are getting it wrong. We definitely need His eye salve to see our true condition on this one. None of us are capable of seeing through the deceitfulness of our hearts on our own.

We all must realize only God can truly access and discern the motives and intents of our hearts correctly, not us. Yes, His Spirit within us can guide us in our motives and reveal to us our errors, but we cannot do this correctly on our own, and if we are not careful, we can unintentionally be hard enough, in our hearts, to block out all His communication within us in such a way that it won't bring forth any fruit in our lives. We can tell ourselves we are doing things in this life to serve God, but somehow we need to factor in the effects of a heart that is more deceitful than all else to really know how much our flesh (selfishness, pride, pleasure, and the like) plays into things. These can be so hidden as to how they play into our decisions, that they make it impossible for us to be honest.

My conclusion is that our understanding and assessment of our motives behind the reasons we do things is corrupt. It is corrupt because of our pride, our selfishness and our hidden desires. Only He can help us see correctly. If we do not approach our walk with a fear of our heart's deceitfulness, we are truly blind. It is so easy to tell ourselves we are serving God, while at the same time refusing to walk in love the way He wants us to. Nothing is hidden from Him. He knows the motives and intents behind our every thought. We all need to turn to Him to show us if there is anything wrong anywhere in our lives. If we are willing to be honest with Him, deep within ourselves, to have a pride broken before Him, then He can and will help us see. If we truly want to walk a walk pleasing to Him, then lets join together in bringing our hearts before Him and ask Him to show us how to walk pleasing to Him. We should all do this today, and we should do this every day, because if there is no fear of error before our eyes related to the possibility of being self deceived, then I am convinced we are already blind and have not comprehended the gravity of the problem we are dealing with, and we are not being led by His Spirit as we could be.

> ***Jer 17:9 "The heart is more deceitful than all else and is desperately sick; Who can understand it?***

I am including this verse again as a reminder, and for further emphasis, that this truth I am trying to share about is not really coming from some great idea on my own, but from a study of my own heart guided by this verse which has convinced me of its truth and its wisdom.

I believe there is a place where we can go in our relationship with Jesus, available for us as believers, where few Christians ever go. The reason I started my sharing with a focus on this possibility of us having a hard heart, and a focus on how the deceitfulness of our heart can blind us to how we really are, is because these two things kept me from having what should have been mine from the start. My testimony is that I walked out almost thirty years, as a believer, blind to my condition. I am writing this in hopes of helping others find what I have found, knowing that I never would have found it if He hadn't opened my eyes to begin to see through this tendency to be blind to the deceitfulness of my own heart. I needed to see how blind, unconscious, hard and callous I was toward the desires of the Lord. If I hadn't seen my true condition, nothing would have changed for me. If we want all He has for us, if we want our full inheritance in the Lord, if we want to go to a place of faith we have never been to before, then we have to face these two issues. Today, if you feel a prick in your heart as you read this, I'm pleading with you to join me in turning to Him and trusting Him with everything that is within you.

I have shared this testimony about the climax of the challenge to my heart in the hope of helping others to find the same place of challenge within their hearts. Every one of us, as believers, has the opportunity to press in closer and closer in our relationship with Jesus. However, there is a hardness and deceitfulness within our hearts toward sin in our lives that limits us. If we truly love Him, we must let Him lead us as we do battle with this condition. We can trust Him to give us the true power to walk in victory. The battle is not really ours at all, but the battle is the Lord's and our part is to step out in faith trusting Him for the victory. As believers, part of the reason we need to trust His way for us is so that He can guide us in how to have victory. I do not know if anyone has ever tested the limits of victory that could be theirs if they could walk in this kind of faith that I see is available to us. Faith that will give us victory over a deceitful and hard heart; over our selfishness; over our self righteous pride; and even over a corrupt thought life. As we learn to trust Him in all the plans He has for us, as we are being conformed to the image of Jesus Christ.

I think all believers want to find a truly genuine faith. I was tired of the complacent kind of faith I had lived with so long. I wanted to find a faith focused on a surrendered walk, caring enough to pay attention and be honest about all that was going on in my heart. I wanted a faith where Jesus was Lord and King and complete obedience to His every wish for me was my command; where a desire to walk pleasing to Him trumps any desire to please myself. At the time I was doing all this questioning, I was wondering if I could be someone who would learn to walk in this kind of faith and who would test the limits of where my faith could go and the change it could bring to my life.

As I made my decision to take this leap, there was not a sense that I knew where this would go, what Jesus would ask of me, what it would cost or how successful I would be. I just felt broken. I was giving up on the thinking that I could understand and reason everything out in advance. I didn't care about all the excuses anymore. I just wanted to see for myself what trusting Jesus and doing things His way would bring. I wanted to delve into what the deepest relationship possible with Jesus might be like. To quote a pastor I heard preach at the time, "I was all in."

Chapter 3

MY LEARNING TO BE LED IN HOW TO WALK WITH JESUS

I described my mindset as "all in" as I started this new walk because I felt a deep sense of surrender to do whatever I believed Jesus would want me to do and I didn't want to care about what that kind of surrender might cost. I wanted to live my life as if I were trying to win the heart of God with how I responded to all He allowed to happen to me. I suppose similar to how one might want to win the heart of someone they loved. I think when we are really trying to win someone's heart; we pay very close attention to how we treat them; we especially care how we respond to anything they ask of us; anything they say to us; we look carefully for any opportunity to do something that they would like. This idea that I was going to win God's heart without considering what it might cost didn't just have me watching what I was doing, I also found myself caring about all the thoughts that went on in my heart. I was watching how I responded or reacted both in thought and deed to all that happened to me. I was even watching how

I responded to little things that I normally might think of as just irritating or frustrating. I knew that God loved me and I didn't really think of this as trying to earn His love. I thought of it more as wanting to learn how to walk in a way that would be pleasing to Him.

As I think back, I realize I had kind of a collection of thoughts as to how I was going to approach what felt to me like a completely new and different walk I wanted to have with Jesus. I don't mean I wrote anything out, but as a believer I think I had something in me that kind of knew what I needed to do. Here is a list of some of the thoughts I had at the time which I felt would help me find that secret place of fellowship I knew was available if I could truly surrender my heart.

> I knew I wanted my number one guidance to be about walking in love, in genuine love, to anyone and everyone at all times. I wanted to be honest with myself and pay close attention, not just to how I treated people, but to how I felt about them. I wanted to be honest about the kind of thoughts that went on in my heart toward others. Was I really feeling a selfless love putting their needs and desires first ahead of my own? Did I really treat them how I wanted to be treated? I knew that the measure of my maturity would have a lot to do with how I felt toward others in my heart.
>
> I wanted to be wise about the possibility of being deceived by my own heart. If I could catch myself being wrong,

I wanted to be quick to spot it and own up to it. I knew if I could see my error, it was going to be because God allowed me to see through my blindness and I wanted to admit it to myself, God and anyone else necessary. I was beginning to understand that I was capable of being blind to seeing my real motives on just about anything I did and blind to my making excuses. I didn't want to defend myself or make excuses anymore.

I wanted to find a new sense of honesty with both God and myself. An honesty about everything that went on in my heart as though what I was thinking was being lived out in His presence and passing before His throne. I knew He didn't want me thinking I could hide anything from Him.

I wanted my understanding of what I thought a true walk of faith would be about to come directly from the Bible. I was going to be very careful to re-examine my thinking as well as being very careful about accepting anyone else's teachings until I was sure it lined up with what the New Testament writers taught. I could see that the New Testament scriptures were written by those God had chosen to help us understand how we were supposed to lives our lives if we wanted to live them pleasing before Him. God was revealing truths, through Jesus Christ, in a new way and they were chosen by Jesus to be enlightened in understanding that way. I also thought of the teachings of Jesus in the gospels as being precious because of how they were full of direct quotes of what He actually said and full of an actual history of things He did. Jesus alone had understood how to live a life perfectly pleasing to the Father in all He said and did. I also found myself hanging intently on every clue I could get from the Old Testament about what God watched for and considered pleasing before Him. It seemed to me that the New Testament writers had gleaned their understanding from all Jesus taught and from all that the Old Testament scriptures taught as they were guided by the way the Holy Spirit was working in their lives to help them understand. As I looked back on how I had studied in the past, I felt like I had studied the Scriptures more to be able to share truths and doctrines with others. Somewhere along the way, I had missed the importance of how they were suppose to affect a change in my heart and the reasons behind why I did things. I had a new sense that I didn't just want to know what Jesus taught, I wanted to figure out how to live my life by those teachings.

I wanted it to be important to see faith as a motive behind everything I did. I wanted to do things as if I were doing them to please Jesus. I wanted faith to be behind how I did things at work as well as how I was toward things when I was just having fun.

I didn't want how I handled possessions, money, time, pride, inconvenience, any of my desires and thoughts about pleasures or anything else to keep me from doing what was right. I wanted to figure out how to handle myself toward all of these areas in a way that would truly be pleasing to Him.

I wanted to understand that nothing I did or thought I needed to accomplish in my life mattered more than living my life for Jesus. Yet, I wanted to understand that how I did everything I did was extremely important. I wanted to care about how I responded to little things as well as big things. I reasoned that nothing should be too small to be important because this was really more about the attitude of my heart toward pleasing Him and the importance of the things that might trigger that attitude weren't what really mattered.

I wanted to be careful to take steps to protect my heart's commitment to follow Jesus every minute of every day by watching and guarding every thought that went on inside me. If my heart started to think about anything that I knew wouldn't be pleasing to Him or wanting to fantasize about any of my old ways, I didn't want to embrace or engage

> any of those thoughts, I wanted to stop that kind of thinking in its tracks. So, if I would catch myself starting to think about something I used to do or how I could work things if I didn't care about trying to understand what Jesus might want me to do, I would stop and affirm to both God and myself that there was no going back to my old ways; back to my "Egypt" and the pleasures of my old life. I was going to try to do this God's way from now on.
>
> I really wanted to try to understand how to seek God with everything that was within me and to understand how to acknowledge Him in all my ways.

I don't find that I feel much different about any of these thoughts today. I still find myself using them to guide my walk each day. I think something in me knew what I needed to do if I was going to walk pleasing before God. My goal was to take myself to a place of faith; to a depth of fellowship with Jesus I had never been to before. I didn't want to settle for just another form of religion. I wanted to find a surrender that would lead me to some place real and I had all these thoughts running in the background of my heart to help guide to that place.

As I look back at my first thirty years as a believer, it has become obvious to me that **"We don't necessarily walk a life pleasing to God just because we have believed in Jesus."** So I want to take some time and share about this third point on my list of truths. I suppose this sounds like a "no brainer" as, of course, it matters to God how we live our lives. But as I look at how I worked my way around this in my own thinking and walk as a believer, I think it is an important point to focus on. I'm not sure just how it happened to me, but I had slipped into a place in my thinking where I reasoned if I tried to be a good Christian, that's all that mattered. No one is perfect but Jesus and He will cover my sins if I get it wrong. Then I defined "good Christian" as reading my Bible regularly, caring about sharing with non-believers how to be saved, fellow-shipping with other believers and spending some time in prayer on a regular basis. These four things had the appearance for me of being a very worthwhile approach to my faith, but the problem was they became the substitute for a changed life and they, in themselves, did not cause a changed life. Selfishness, anxiety, pride, anger, malice, coveting, lust, judging others, withholding love from whomever I wanted and however I wanted all could be going on in my walk at the same time as I met my definition of a "good Christian." Nothing about my walk as a "good Christian" was helping to either curb the desires of my flesh or preventing me from carrying out the deeds of my flesh. If I looked at the surface, sure, my life looked changed enough. But the truth is when I looked at what was going on inside me, in my heart; it really wasn't much different than before I got saved. If how we live our lives during our stay upon this earth really does matter, then don't we need to be very careful and honest about the kind of life we are living, including what goes on in our hearts?

There seems to be the thinking in a lot of the Christian circles I've been around that if we have really believed then, of course, we will live our lives pleasing to God. Sometimes it seems like it's an accepted fundamental doctrine of faith, but as far as I am concerned, as a believer looking at how I have been able to live my life, I have unequivocally proved this sort of thinking false. I am confident that if anyone reading this were to be honest about how they really are and what goes on in their hearts, they would understand they have proved it false as well. The conclusion I have come to is that it matters how I live my life. My attitude toward every thought of my heart matters. If, as believers, we want to live our lives in a way that is pleasing to God, the most important conclusion I think we can come to is that we have to include being honest about how we are and about what goes on inside of us.

All the things I was doing to be a "good Christian", including the sacrifices, so to speak, I was making, were not what Jesus really wanted from me. What He really wanted was a heart that was full of faith and trust; a heart that cared about trying to respond to things in a way that would truly be pleasing to Him. He wanted me to trust that I could live my life to please Him and not myself and it would be OK. In fact, He wanted me to have a faith where I believed it was not just OK, but a faith where I understood it would really be the best way to live my life. I was beginning to see that this kind of approach to the Christian walk is really the only way I was going to learn how to walk pleasing before Him.

The conclusion I've come to is that if I want to live my life pleasing before God, it really needs to be about my whole life. It needs to be about everything I do; every response I choose. These reflect something about the attitude of my heart and since He doesn't just care about what I do; what He really cares about is my heart's attitude and motives as I do it. My hope in sharing this is to challenge and encourage all of us to approach our walks in a more conscience and caring way. As believers, not everything about this walk is automatic. We really do need to care about learning how to live our lives in a way that is pleasing before God. If today, these truths have touched your heart and you feel challenged, I hope you will join me in a way of walking out a commitment to an honesty of heart before God and an intentional sincerity of faith that's ever growing as we walk with Jesus our Lord. May we all be known as those who are after the heart of God.

Chapter 4

ALL THE THOUGHTS OF MY HEART ARE LIVED OUT BEFORE HIS THRONE

In my new walk, I found myself awaking each day with my first thoughts being about living this day to please the Lord. I was growing in the understanding that He was aware of everything that I was going through no matter how important or minor it seemed. He knew every test that was going to come this day and I wanted to go through every test with the desire to handle it in a way that was pleasing to Him. I was realizing that He either designed the test just for me, or was making whatever test happened work out for my benefit. It seemed to me that He cared more about how I handled the test than what the test was He might allow. I had the sense that He was watching my thoughts and my heart response to each interaction I went through during the day. If I was going to "pass the test" so to speak, then I would have to respond in my heart to any test that came in a way that would be pleasing to Him.

I was beginning to understand that it wasn't just

what I did that He cared about, but that He cared about why I did things and every thought that went on in my heart as I did them. I know that all of us have come up with our own way of traveling through this life making decisions and thinking thoughts in a way that works and seems right to us. Most of us see ourselves as basically good people, or as I thought about myself as basically a good Christian, but as I have studied the scriptures both in the old and the new Testaments it has become more and more obvious to me that God cares more about what is going on in my heart than what I actually do. I was coming to the conclusion that if I wanted to live a life pleasing to Him, then I needed to care about what was going on in my heart too. Every thought really did matter. I want to share a couple of verses that served to drive this home in my thinking. This is from David, at the end of his life, sharing perhaps this final thought with his son Solomon:

> ***1 Chr 28:9 "As for you, my son Solomon, know the God of your father, and serve Him with a whole heart and a willing mind; for the LORD searches all hearts, and understands every intent of the thoughts. If you seek Him, He will let you find Him ..."***

Over the years, I have come to understand that there was something special going on between David and God. I'm sure all of us would like the assessment of our walk that David got from God "that he was a man after God's heart." If you are like me, you probably watch carefully for clues as to how David gained this assessment. So here we have David sharing one final piece of wisdom with Solomon. What if we as Christians approached our walks with the mindset and the wisdom that we were going to serve God with a whole heart and with a willing mind? Knowing that He searches our hearts and minds and He knows the intents of our every thought, what would that kind of a walk look like? David, in the way he said this, seems to be witnessing to Solomon. But if you check the context, you will find he was also witnessing to all Israel as he had assembled them for the official coronation of Solomon. However, as I read this, I realized David was reaching across thousands of years and was witnessing to me. To us. This is just as much true today as it was when he said it to Solomon.

If we are going to have a truly sincere faith, then the truths we learn should have an effect on us. If we really believe that our thoughts are played out in the presence of God as David concluded, then don't we also have to conclude that our thoughts matter and the intents or motives behind those thoughts matter?

I know the way we think God judges things is not something we talk about much as believers. But behind the thought that something matters to God should be the understanding that it matters because God judges it. There is no other reason to think it would matter. If we say that He sees something, aren't we also at the same time implying He judges it? Once again, why else even mention "He sees it" if we are not thinking He is going to judge it? As believers, we know that someday we will all stand before the judgment seat of Christ. We will answer for anything that matters about how we have walked our lives and what we have done with His teachings. We will give an account for how we have lived our lives. "Nothing is hidden from Him." There is not one thought that passes through our minds or our hearts, but that He sees both the thought and the motive behind the thought. If you are feeling a little "undone" by the idea of this kind of an all inclusive judgment, then I expect you are on the verge of understanding what it means.

This undone feeling of helplessness that begins with the thought, "I can't fix this", should take us to the next thought as a believer, "Jesus help me." I think perhaps our biggest problem as believers may well be that we think we can walk this life without a sincere faith and somehow we still conclude that it's all OK. But what if what God wants from us is to admit we can't fix our hearts? What if what He wants is for us to find a faith where we trust Him to fix it? Not the thinking that our thoughts don't matter and not the thinking that I can fix myself and that will be good enough for God's judgment in the way I handle things. But getting to a place where we give up on our own efforts and start trusting by faith that He will fix us. I am convinced that He really does have a plan, and at the heart of that plan lays the importance of how we walk daily with Jesus.

When talking about judgment for believers, I think we need to keep in mind that we have already passed out of death into life; we are hidden in Christ; He has paid our debt for us. Jesus Christ is the cornerstone of our faith and He is the foundation in our lives, but it's what we chose to build on this foundation that matters at the judgment seat of Christ. If we love Jesus and we obey His ways for us (His commandments), then we are walking pleasing before the Father bearing fruit during this life and storing up treasures and rewards for ourselves that will last for all eternity.

But if we turn a hard heart to God's ways for us, we are wasting the opportunity of a life time to bring glory to Jesus in how we choose to live our lives. I see that we bring glory to Jesus when we are obedient in surrendering to follow His direction and plan that He has for our lives. His way for us comes to us through the Holy Spirit He has made to dwell in us. It brings glory because of the power He will provide to walk in His way and because of the fruit His way will produce as we walk led by His Word He has implanted in our hearts. Our changed lives as we mature under the leading of His Holy Spirit proves God's love for us in that He provided this opportunity for us through the death of His Son on the cross. It shows His faithfulness because He is always there to guide us in His way. So when we talk about the judgment of believers, we are looking at how we conduct ourselves during our time on this earth, (including all that goes on in our hearts) as we walk surrendered to His way and His plan He has for us. Hebrews talks about the blessing we will receive if we get this right or the lack of blessing if we get it wrong in this way:

> *Heb 6:7-9 For ground that drinks the rain which often falls on it and brings forth vegetation useful to those for whose sake it is also tilled, receives a blessing from God; but if it yields thorns and thistles, it is worthless and close to being cursed, and it ends up being burned.*
>
> *But, beloved, we are convinced of better things concerning you, and things*

that accompany salvation, though we are speaking in this way.

So on my list of truths I am sharing, this is how I see this fourth truth played out for us. **"It is not just the action that we do that matters, but it is the thoughts and intents of our hearts that lay behind those actions that really matters."** I think this truth is charged with another challenge for anyone who has been given a heart to see it. Today, if this has touched you as truth, I urge you to commit to yourself to be more conscious caring and honest before God about all that goes on in your heart. I am convinced that this has to be an element of any sincere faith, and that this commitment alone will turn any kind of walk we may have into a sincere walk that starts from the moment we wake from sleep and continues throughout the day. It is a walk filled with faith because of the understanding that our life, even our thought life, is lived out in the presence of God.

Chapter 5

TRUSTING HIM TO SHOW ME MY HURTFUL WAYS

Now I had gotten to a place in my heart where I could truly say, "I want to walk a life pleasing to Jesus." I was thinking to myself, I'm going to deal with my selfishness, my pride, my desire for the things of this world and I'm going to learn to walk in love just as Jesus would want me to. I have already shared with you, back in chapter three, the lofty goals of the heart I had running in the background of my thoughts, but as I set out on this quest, one of the things I realized right away was I often didn't see the influences of selfishness, pride, or desires until after they had already tainted the way I responded to something. I could want not to be affected by these, but I was quickly coming to the conclusion that I couldn't, on my own, just suddenly not be influenced by them. In fact, I was so used to their influences, that I was often just blind to see their inter-workings in the way I responded to things.

I would wander off in thought about something and then realize the selfish motivation behind the thought, or I would catch myself thinking about something and then see how invested in self pride my thoughts were. As I was trying to be honest and conscious about my thinking, I was becoming more and more aware of the negative influences that selfishness, pride and the like had on my life. Unexpectedly, something very special was beginning to happen for me. Because I wanted to set the motives of my heart on pleasing the Lord, I could see that recognizing these negative influences and facing them head on was the approach to my walk that would be pleasing to the Lord. Under the hardness of my old approach, I hadn't cared enough to bother to want to see them. However, pressing myself to walk pleasing to Him now meant that removing the negative influences in my response to my various trials was exactly what did please Him. Something else very special that I was becoming aware of was that the Lord was opening my eyes to see the workings of my flesh in the way I responded to the test He brought into my life.

I want to pause here and give my definition of what I mean when I use the term flesh. It is a term I have already been using and I know I will want to use the term flesh more as we go along. So, I think it is worthwhile to explain what I mean when I use it. For years I thought of the Biblical use of the term flesh as somewhat confined to sexual lust, but I have come to realize it is much more than that. I see the workings of the flesh as the complex interaction between the physical desires we have and our selfishness, pride and desires for both the physical and material things of life. This is not to say that every physical desire is wrong, but I think the Biblical understanding of the workings of the flesh would be the corruption of the physical desires as a result of the inter-workings of selfishness, pride, lust and the like. I was beginning to wake up to the understanding that putting to death the deeds and desires of my flesh was exactly what a walk pleasing to the Lord was suppose to look like. Now that He was helping me to see the influences of my flesh, there was a new hope of being able to overcome their power over me.

I suppose it should be obvious that if we are blind to our selfishness, we won't be able to overcome its influences. If we can't see our pride, we won't be able to keep it from affecting how we respond to various trials. If we are unable to see our greed, our lust, our anger or any of the other workings of our flesh, we would never be able to overcome their influences. But if our walks could take on this new dimension I was experiencing, of being shown my selfishness or any of the other influences of my flesh, and if our hearts are set on trying to please Him, we can find victory through Him over their power in our lives.

It seems to me that if we think the various facets that the flesh can take on are having no influence in our lives just because we don't see them, we are foolish and deceived. As I see it, the entire goal of our walk with Jesus is to become mature enough, wise enough, trained as it were, that we learn to put to death the constant pressures that come from the flesh. I think wisdom on this is knowing that our hearts tend to be blind to the workings of the flesh and that we need the Lord to give us a heart to see if we are going to see. If we are truly set in our thinking that we want to please Him, then we should be delighted if He is helping us to see our selfishness, our pride, or any of the other workings of our flesh.

When I started my new way of walking with Him, what I noticed was, as I went throughout my day reacting to the little things that were happening to me, I began to understand that these things were happening to me as various trials or tests that would reveal to me the condition of my heart. If I was upset by a trial, then I could know that anger was in my heart. If I was anxious about something, then I could know I wasn't trusting God as I should. If some test God allowed brought thoughts of lust, then I was being tested by lust and my lust was being exposed. I would see glimpses of the workings of the flesh in my thinking. When I was honest enough to see my heart being influenced by my flesh, I found myself saying to the Lord, "Lord I don't want to be selfish, I want to be like Jesus," or "I don't want to be run by pride, I want to be like Jesus," or "I don't want to be driven by lust, I want to be like your Son." I knew if I could respond to things in my heart like Jesus did, I would be walking in a way that would be pleasing to the Father. We know Jesus was tested just like us by all the things of this world but He always responded in a way that was pleasing to the Father. The biggest difference in this new approach to my walk was I was not thinking I knew how to be righteous or good, but quite the opposite. I knew I couldn't see through the deceitfulness of my heart reliably, so my goal became to try to understand how He wanted me to respond to whatever trial He let happen and obey that understanding. I was learning that I might not know how to be righteous, but I could understand how to be obedient.

I want to insert the 5th on my list of truths I am sharing about here. I think this is as plain and concise as I can put it. **"We can try to see how we are on our own, but because of how deceptive our hearts are, we need God to guide our every step."** We need to have an honest heart before Him to make this work. It is useless to think we can be guided by Him if we are anything less than honest before Him. If He is showing us the workings of our flesh in the way we react to test or trials, what good would it be if we are not honest enough to acknowledge our faults? Being honest enough to see what He is trying to show us is the first step in walking in a way that is pleasing to Him.

Here is another example of something David did that we learn about in the Psalms.

> ***Ps 139:23-24 Search me, O God, and know my heart; Try me and know my anxious thoughts; And see if there be any hurtful way in me, And lead me in the everlasting way.***

I say something David did, not just something he said, because I think David genuinely wanted God to show him his faults and to guide him in how to walk pleasing before Him. David seems to have understood that he might not see his anxious thoughts or his hurtful ways on his own. He understood that he needed God to guide him. If you have set your heart on trying to understand how to have a walk pleasing to our Lord, then I am sure you can see the importance in this 5th truth. In finding a walk that is pleasing to Jesus, we should always have running in the background of our thinking, in the depths of our heart, this same prayer that David walked with in his heart. "Search me, know me, try me, test me, let me see my hurtful ways so I can deal with them; let me be guided by You Lord as You lead me in the everlasting way".

My prayer both for myself and for anyone reading this is that God will help us all have a heart to see the importance of learning to be guided by Jesus in how to find a walk pleasing to the Father. I hope you feel challenged enough to embrace this truth right now, today. If you commit your heart to being led by Jesus so that you can walk pleasing to Him, He will be faithful to lead and guide you in every step you walk. We just need to let Him do this for us. We can walk led by the Spirit of Christ within us today and we can continue to be led by His Spirit for all the days of our life. I hope you are beginning to get a glimpse of the wonder and the depths of the opportunity that is open for any and all believers as we walk out our lives for all the world to see.

Chapter 6

TRYING TO UNDERSTAND HOW HIS SPIRIT LEADS ME

I think I walked most of my first thirty years of being a Christian with the understanding that I knew I should try to be nice to people. I knew I was supposed to love everyone. But without having my eyes opened by His Spirit to see how I really was, the influences of being led by my flesh unknowingly affected my every response. I can see now in looking back, that I had never been able to accomplish treating people with a genuine love the way Jesus really would have wanted me to because I couldn't see through my selfishness, pride, lustful desires, or any of the influences of my flesh without His help. Now, as I sought to walk in a genuine love toward others, I understood that if I could find His leading in the way He would guide me to respond in love, my response would be uncontaminated by the influences of my flesh and be the perfect way to respond. As I tried to follow His ways for me, I realized I was being trained to see what a response, led by my flesh, would look like, and what a response led by the Holy Spirit would look like. I was learning that if I wanted to walk pleasing to Jesus, I had to choose His Spirit led response.

I suppose it would be interesting to try to keep track of how many decisions we make in a day, where love could be seen as part of our response and the underlying motive behind that response, if we do things God's way. I don't think there is ever an interaction between people where we could look and not see the possibility for love to be behind how we might respond. In my new walk, I had set my heart on trying to see how to respond in love to everyone, everywhere and every time. I think an approach of trying to be led by "what would love do" is at heart a good approach. The only flaw in thinking this, would be if we try to do it without His leading. My inability to understand what genuine love might look like in any given situation on my own without Jesus' help was why I had gotten it so wrong in the past. The influences of my flesh were such that I was realizing that I would always need His guidance if I was going to get love right in the way I responded. I couldn't naturally get it right on my own. This new walk provided the fix as long as I surrendered to wanting His leading and choosing in obedience to follow that leading in the way I responded.

Since I started this new walk, I have also been studying the inter-workings of what I have seen as going on in my heart and the changes this whole experience has brought about for me. In the first months, I reasoned that God was fixing my heart by changing it. In a way this was true, but not like I thought it would be. I guess I thought He was going to make it more righteous and remove its deceptive nature. I thought it was about purging it of lust, greed, selfishness and the like in such a way that I wouldn't even have to deal with them at some point. But as time passed, I began to realize my new walk didn't exactly change the nature of my heart. I could see it was about me looking at the choices set before me; both the way I would let my heart think about things and the way I would let myself respond to things. I knew at any moment I could still respond to things in my old way of unconsciously being influenced or led by lust, greed, selfishness, or any of the workings of my flesh, so I don't think the nature of my heart was really changed. I discovered it was more that my heart was being trained to know His way of loving; trained to look at itself, to see it's tendency toward sin; and then if I desired to walk in a way that pleased Him, I would want to overcome that tendency by the choices I would make. As long as I let His Spirit lead me, I could be confident that the direction was righteous and not contaminated by the influences of my flesh. I see it more as that my heart was being trained by His Spirit to trust Him to lead me and as I was led, I was becoming trained to care and believe that how I responded, within my heart, to anything and everything mattered. My new heart, if I think of it that way, was different in that it cared about knowing what way of responding would be pleasing to Him and by faith I knew if I truly sought His way He would help me and let me find it. So the real fixing that was happening was not about changing the nature of my flesh or even the tendency of my heart toward deception. That part of my nature still seemed to be the same. But as my heart was being trained, I was learning that if I wanted to walk pleasing to Him, what I needed to do was to acknowledge and surrender to His leading. If I tried to respond without His leading, the motives behind my response were always going to be a little corrupt.

In a way, there was a testing of my heart that went on all day long, because there were conversations going on in my heart all the time. I now was aware that all the thoughts of my heart were happening in the presence of God. I understood that every single one of these conversations mattered. But within the idea of the direction of each thought of my heart being a test that gave both myself and God a read on where my heart was at in its maturity, lie the opportunity for my heart to respond in a way that showed victory over the influences of the flesh; the opportunity to respond to that test in a way pleasing to God. If I was honest and learned to respond in my heart the way He would want me to, then I would pass the test (so to speak), but His tests were exposing the influences of a lifetime of unconsciously walking led by lust, greed, selfishness, pride and the like. A sense of loathing as to what I was like on my own, and how truly blind I was without Him, was moving me into a greater dependence on His leading each day that passed.

It seemed the more He would allow me to see my own heart, the more I was realizing the depths of the problem. There was a growing sense of how utterly incapable I was of seeing the influences my flesh had on the decisions I made under my own guidance. I was becoming aware that there were two sources of guidance I could draw from within me. One was my own way of thinking and processing through my mind that was contaminated by the influences of my flesh, and the other being led by the Spirit of Christ within my heart. The flesh led response seemed to be my default setting, and the only way I managed to not be led by my flesh was if I was being led by His Spirit.

I'm going to cite a couple of verses here that I see parallel this conclusion that I think may explain it better than I can. I want to include both a quote from Romans and one from Galatians that I consider important encouragement for me in my understanding of this walk.

> *Rom 8:5-8 For those who are according to the flesh set their minds on the things of the flesh, but those who are according to the Spirit, the things of the Spirit. For the mind set on the flesh is death, but the mind set on the Spirit is life and peace, because the mind set on the flesh is hostile toward God; for it does not subject itself to the law of God, for it is not even able {to do so,} and those who are in the flesh cannot please God.*
>
> *Gal 5:16-25 But I say, walk by the Spirit, and you will not carry out the desire of the flesh. For the flesh sets its desire against the Spirit, and the Spirit against the flesh; for these are in opposition to one another, so that you may not do the things that you please. But if you are led by the Spirit, you are not under the Law. Now the deeds of the flesh are evident, which are: immorality, impurity, sensuality, idolatry, sorcery, enmities, strife, jealousy, outbursts of anger, disputes, dissensions, factions, envying, drunkenness, carousing, and things like*

> ***these, of which I forewarn you, just as I have forewarned you, that those who practice such things will not inherit the kingdom of God. But the fruit of the Spirit is love, joy, peace, patience, kindness, goodness, faithfulness, gentleness, self-control; against such things there is no law. Now those who belong to Christ Jesus have crucified the flesh with its passions and desires. If we live by the Spirit, let us also walk by the Spirit.***

Paul, in both of these quotes, emphasizes the importance of this idea of setting the mind and the heart on being led by the Spirit and in this last comment, "Let us also walk by the Spirit," is implied the truth that this is a choice we need to make. It implies, as I have concluded, that it is not automatic just because I have believed, been saved, and sealed by His Spirit. I am trying to explain, as clearly as I can, what it means to me to be led by the Spirit of Christ within me. To help you understand how His leading happens for me, I want you to know that I do not necessarily see, in an intellectual way, a clear distinction between the directions that I understand as coming from the Holy Spirit, and the directions that come from the thoughts of my own conscience, mind and heart. I believe this is because He is speaking His ways directly to my mind and my heart. But as I walk this leading out by faith, on a spiritual level, I do know with certainty, the leading that is coming from Him. Because of the way His Spirit works in my heart, it is often His written word that makes me so sure and gives me guidance as to how I should respond in a way that would be truly pleasing to Him. I think if we are truly wanting to know His way, we need to listen very carefully to how the written words from the Bible speaks to our conscience about what is the right way to respond from our heart. I have noticed so often that His Spirit brings to light guidance for me through verses that are brought into my thoughts if I will look for them. I want to be wise in how I understand this because I know there are ways that the heart can twist the written word to manipulate situations, but I can be sure because of the way His Spirit leads, that as I follow Him, I will be able to distinguish between directions, which come from the Spirit of Christ within me and that which is from my flesh or another source. His ways will sit in my heart as good, pure, righteous, always full of genuine love that is willing to be self sacrificing and my heart will want to do it to please Him even if it is in secret from the rest of the world. I think that our hearts really do delight to do His will when we know His way. As I think about how I see His leading happen in my heart, it is interesting to consider Jesus' teaching in these verses from John.

> *John 10:4-5 "When he puts forth all his own, he goes ahead of them, and the sheep follow him because they know his voice. "A stranger they simply will not follow, but will flee from him, because they do not know the voice of strangers."*
>
> *John 10:27-28 "My sheep hear My voice, and I know them, and they follow Me; and I give eternal life to them, and they will never perish; and no one will snatch them out of My hand.*

I hope you will bear with me for what I consider a bit of scripturally backed reasoning here, as I attempt to explain my thoughts on what I think the voice of the Spirit within our hearts is all about. Here is a thought I want us to consider as we go through some verses. Are we any less obligated to keep His commandments, His ways, His Words, His teachings, or obey His leading's just because we can't easily see intellectually the source of His way for us? I think if we are going to have a sincere walk of faith that is bent on pleasing Him, somehow we have to get past a heart that is hard enough that it looks for excuses to not deal with the flesh. If this leading of His Spirit is happening in our hearts, then no matter how subtle it might seem, we are still obligated to follow it if we want to think we are going to walk pleasing to Him. My experience is that part of the reason His leading seems subtle and obscure is actually because of our hard hearts, and as our hearts are broken of this hardness by following the Holy Spirit's leading, His leading becomes easier and easier to find and understand.

Here are a couple of verses that have helped me come to these conclusions. The first is in John.

> John 7:37-39 *"Now on the last day, the great {day} of the feast, Jesus stood and cried out, saying, "If anyone is thirsty, let him come to Me and drink. "He who believes in Me, as the Scripture said, 'From his innermost being will flow rivers of living water.'" But this He spoke of the Spirit, whom those who believed in Him were to receive; for the Spirit was not*

yet {given,} because Jesus was not yet glorified."

Jesus is telling us as He cries out, that if we believe in Him, something special is going to happen; that from our inner most being will flow rivers of living water. I don't think we would really know what He was talking about if it weren't for John adding the comment that explains it. Jesus was talking about the Spirit that would be given to all believers after He was glorified. All believers, being us, you and me. If we have believed in Him, then we can know we are among those who were to receive this Spirit He promised, "To give to anyone who believed in Him." I think that we can conclude from this, that if we have believed in Him, we can, in fact, rest in the confidence that He has indeed given us the Spirit as He promised. Secondly, I think we can know that from our innermost being are flowing rivers of living water. I suppose the question of exactly what this living water is all about leaves a bit of a mystery. I take it to be referring to some sort of communication from the Spirit happening within us. I also think "river" suggests the abundance of communication that is available. If we accept that this is happening to all believers, why isn't it more obvious? Can it be flowing in us right now, and yet at the same time we do not realize it's happening? The answer for me is, I do believe this is happening within my heart right now, it is not something I can prove to anyone else, but it is a communication I have access to as a believer. I know that I have to accept it by faith because its nature is spiritual and not obvious. I want to point out here that just because it isn't easily tangible to our thinking, does not mean it isn't happening.

The next verse I wanted to share is from the book of Hebrews and it speaks of a new covenant that God is going to make with His people.

> ***Heb 8:10 "FOR THIS IS THE COVENANT THAT I WILL MAKE WITH THE HOUSE OF ISRAEL AFTER THOSE DAYS, SAYS THE LORD: I WILL PUT MY LAWS INTO THEIR MINDS, AND I WILL WRITE THEM ON THEIR HEARTS. AND I WILL BE THEIR GOD, AND THEY SHALL BE MY PEOPLE.***

As Christians, I think most of us agree, and even celebrate in our thinking, that we are not under the Law as Israel was. But with the advent of Christ, we have moved into a new covenant and this verse out of the book of Hebrew's, (a quote from the Old Testament) provides a cornerstone for much of our understanding of this new covenant. But this promise, "I will put My laws into their minds and I will write them on their hearts," what does this mean? It seems to me it is a similar and parallel thought to what Jesus talked about in reference to the "Living Water." So if we (as believers) are under the New Covenant (as I believe we are) then God is now speaking His Laws directly to our hearts and our minds. In asking myself if this is happening, once again, the answer for me as a believer is, if this is happening right now for me, it is not something I can prove to anyone else? I do think His communications flow like a living water from my inner most being, but I know that I have to accept this by faith because its nature is spiritual and not obvious. I also want to point out once again that just because it isn't easily tangible to our thinking, does not mean it isn't happening.

So here is the thought for us. What if exactly as promised, that with Jesus, we have moved into a new covenant, and now God, through the Spirit of Christ within us, is speaking His ways to our hearts and our minds, but it is subtle and not controlling? What if this "Word of God" actually is like a river flowing from our inner most being and in God's wisdom it is intended to cleanse us from all unrighteousness as it trains us and guides us in how to walk a life pleasing before Him, but all it takes to choke out this leading and make it fruitless is a hard heart? That is, a heart focused a little too much on pride, money, pleasure, the deceitfulness of riches or any of the worries of this world; a heart led by the flesh instead of the Spirit of Christ. What if all these can choke out His word in such a way that even though the Words of Christ are being spoken directly to our hearts and our minds, they end up not bearing any fruit?

Is it really so inconceivable to us that God would make this about us having to choose? Jesus had a teaching about wisdom, related to choosing to act upon His words that seems to apply perfectly here. If we hear His words and we choose to act on them, then we would be considered wise, but if we just hear His words and they bring forth no fruit, because of how our hearts are, then we shall be considered foolish.

> *Matt 7:24-27 "Therefore everyone who hears these words of Mine and acts on them, may be compared to a wise man who built his house on the rock. "And the rain fell, and the floods came, and the*

> ***winds blew and slammed against that house; and {yet} it did not fall, for it had been founded on the rock. "Everyone who hears these words of Mine and does not act on them, will be like a foolish man who built his house on the sand. "The rain fell, and the floods came, and the winds blew and slammed against that house; and it fell--and great was its fall."***

This is my perspective on this truth as I have looked as honestly at my own heart as I can. I believe that for the first thirty years of my walk as a Christian, God was indeed speaking His ways to both my heart and my mind. He had made available to me, through the Spirit within me, this guidance and teaching about how to walk pleasing before Him. But because I was blind to it, it was veiled enough to bring forth little or no fruit. The tragedy for me is that I could have been walking in a Godly love that was coming from being led by Christ, but because of my ignorance, I walked in a love tainted by self righteous motives and guided by my own corrupt reasoning and it was so influenced by the way my flesh works that it could never please God.

I did not start what I have been calling "a new way of walking" with any idea of where it was going to take me. I wanted to understand how to truly live my life in a way that was pleasing to Jesus. But where this has taken me I could never have foreseen. When I started, I did not have any understanding of the kind of leading by His Spirit that was available to me; of the depths of the intimate fellowship with God through His Spirit that would happen; of what a difference a truly sincere faith would be like; or the power for walking in victory that could be mine. I feel a little like I'm on the other side of an understanding I stumbled upon, shouting back at everyone: "This way! This way!" But most can't seem to understand what I'm talking about because they have no more reference to help them see the possibilities of where this walk can go than I did. The entrance to this side of understanding all this, for me, seems to have been actions based on my faith, not understanding based on intellect. This walk has turned out to be a faith perfected by works in a walk where works that have incorrect motives are useless and dead. I feel like I stumbled into this new place of surrender when my walk became truly based on faith. I know that I have only began to see the depth of the riches of the inheritance that belong to me and to all of us who have believed in Jesus, but my plea for anyone reading this is, search for this place, this hidden mystery of God, this understanding, this inheritance, because if you have believed you have His Spirit and it belongs to you.

I am once again going to try to be as clear as I can. I am convinced that **God has made a way to guide us, through His Spirit He has put within us, that will lead us correctly in love every time.** How tragic is the thought that we can walk a lifetime as Christians (even serious Christians) and never discover this truth. We can think we have need of nothing believing that we are walking out our lives pleasing to God in every way, while at the same time being blind to our own hard hearts. We come into truth however we come into it, and we come into it whenever we come into it. So if today your heart is moved in such a way that you can see and hear this truth, I hope you will be moved enough to intentionally seek after His guidance with all your heart, with all your mind and with everything that is within you. I am sure of this promise: that if you seek Him with all your heart, He will let you find Him. ***Heb 11:6 ... He is a rewarder of those who seek Him.***

I know it doesn't matter to God if we have walked in ignorance for a lifetime or whether we just got saved. Today, if you hear His voice in your heart, turn to Him and He will lead you for the rest of your days. Whether you are young and have years ahead of you, or you are sick and now you have only days left to live, I hope you will turn to Jesus, find a place of surrender in your heart and let Him lead you for the rest of your life. I know that one day walking led by the Spirit of Christ within us, is more precious than a lifetime lived any other way.

Chapter 7

FINDING A SENSE OF FULFILLMENT IN EVERY AREA OF MY LIFE

In my walk, during the first thirty years of being a Christian, I created a sense of division in my thinking, between my spiritual life and my work/play life. I slipped into a place where the time spent doing Christian things like going to church, Bible studies, listening to teaching programs, reading Christian books, listening to Christian music or any of the other Christian type things all felt spiritual. But work or play did not normally fall into the category of what seemed like time spent with the Lord. I probably envied a little those who managed to find a way to turn their work into part of their walk by having a "service to the Lord" oriented job. I know I occasionally found ways to make work and play feel like they had a spiritual side to them, but most of the time they seemed pretty worldly. If I found the opportunity to share the gospel with someone, of course that felt good, but the sense of spiritual division I had created always left me with a little tinge of guilt about the fact that I worked at such a common field as construction. I don't mean to say I didn't like my work. I actually enjoyed my work and I was proud of the fact that I tried to do my work based on Christian principles. I liked the feeling of accomplishment I had when I looked back at the end of each day and saw the physical evidence of what we had completed as a company. Still, there existed a sense of division toward areas I considered religious and part of my Christian walk and a sense of being part of the world in the other areas of my life. I didn't exactly think of myself as a bad Christian as a result of this spiritual division, but it left me with a sense that my life at work was not being lived as purposeful as it could be and I had a bit of an unfulfilled longing because of it.

I have shared about this sense of spiritual division I had during the first years of my Christian walk because I think most serious Christians share with me, to some degree, this same sense of spiritual division. The thinking that those in full time Christian service are in the front lines and we who have settled for regular jobs have stayed behind the lines in some sort of support capacity has been a common understanding in most of the Christian circles I have been around. The underlying sense that this way of thinking built in the back of my mind caused me to feel a little stuck in a somewhat useless job because I couldn't figure out how to enter full time service. I think this sense of division, in the long run, is extremely damaging to our walks and is caused by a bit of a twisted understanding of what our Christian walk really should be. I think the twist comes from the thinking that the Christian walk is about doing Christian things instead of the understanding that our walk is about being led and trained by the Spirit of Christ within us at any and every moment in time.

My observation on this in my own life is that since I started living my life focused on being trained by the Spirit, the sense of a separation in different areas of my life has all but vanished for me. I now realize that no matter what I'm doing or where I am doing it, I am in the center of the plan Jesus has for my life. Everything that is happening around me and to me is part of that plan. And every moment of my life is important to the Lord because I am being trained and led by the Spirit to walk in love to those around me. The sense that if I am walking in this manner, it is the most I can do to walk pleasing before God has changed how I feel toward both work and play. It is my witness of a walk of faith to all the people around me. Walking in obedience to the Holy Spirit really is the most I can do with my life to help anyone. This has also made it easy for me to share about Jesus with non believers verbally when I get the chance, because I already feel like I'm sharing about my faith with them, in the way I walk led by Jesus as I interact with them. My hope is that even if I don't seem to have an opportunity to share with others verbally how to walk by faith or be saved by faith, perhaps I might win them to a place where they want to know more as I walk my faith out before them. The most important thing for me to do is genuinely interact with love toward people in a way that is pleasing to God. Whether I ever get an open door to share verbally or not, is really in God's control anyway. As I interact with believers in my life, I also have the hope that I will encourage them to walk in obedience to the word of the Spirit within themselves as they observe how I walk my life. I understand now that because God cares intimately about every second of my life no matter where I am or what I'm doing that there really is no division and separation to the different types of things I do; there is only walking in fellowship with Jesus through the Spirit He has made to dwell in me. This understanding has brought a sense of purpose, victory and fulfillment into every area of my life that is almost beyond comprehension.

I know we are admonished throughout the scriptures to live our lives for Jesus, so I want to share this teaching from Peter that often encourages me when I think of it as I walk throughout the day. It seems to me a very clear teaching as he reminds us that our walks can be precious in the sight of God. I know Peter is specifically speaking to wives in this verse, but I think the thought of winning someone to obedience to the word, by the way we live our lives, carries across the board to any and all relationships we might have. I hope you can see, as I have seen, that if we say we love someone and want to win them to the Lord, then how we walk in love toward them really does matter.

> ***1 Pet 3:1-4 ... so that even if any {of them} are disobedient to the word, they may be won without a word by the behavior of their wives, as they observe your chaste and respectful behavior. ... but {let it be} the hidden person of the heart, with the imperishable quality of a gentle and quiet spirit, which is precious in the sight of God ...***

When my focus changed from doing "Christian things" to caring about what was going on in my heart, I started to wake up to see that what He wanted from me was a heart completely surrendered to being trained and led by Him, and the doing of "Christian things" needed to fall under that same surrender or they were of little value. I could see that He cared about **every** response that went on in my heart **at all times.** I think it is the **"at all times"** part of this that changed my understanding about divisions between the Christian things and the work/play part of my life. I could now see that being trained by the Holy Spirit in how to walk pleasing to Jesus was what really mattered and that it was a 24/7 thing. If I was going to walk led by Jesus, it was going to happen **anywhere** I went and it was going to be happening **no matter what I was doing.** It was going on when I was playing and it didn't matter what kind of playing that was. It was going to be happening while I was working and it didn't matter what kind of work I was doing. And yes, it would be happening while I did "Christian things" and it didn't matter what kind of "Christian things" they were. The most important thing in my life was to try to live it in such a way that it would be pleasing to God and I could now see that this kind of understanding made my whole life into a spiritual walk. Everything I did was part of my witness before the Father as to who Christ was to me, and any fruit I might bear was a result of Jesus' leading and His power.

So this is how I've written the seventh truth on my list of truths I'm sharing about here.

We can be led by His Spirit in how to respond to all that goes on in our heart, both how to deal with

our thoughts themselves, and how to respond in love to those around us.

If Jesus is our Lord, if He is our master, if He really is our king, then let's crown Him king in our hearts and let Him lead us in how we walk out love in every aspect of our lives and at all times. I think this is our true spiritual service of worship. I want to be as clear here as I can in saying, "that this leading of the Spirit of Christ is equally available to every believer at all times." We don't need to become a pastor, or a missionary or any other full time service to the Lord related job to have access to it. We can choose to be led by His Spirit right here, right now. The commandments of Christ are in our very hearts. This is not too difficult for us nor is it out of reach for any of us. Jesus has said, "For My yoke is easy and My burden is light." Jesus way He would have us walk is near us. It is in our very hearts so that we can follow it. Today, let us turn to Jesus with all our heart and all our soul and everything that is within us and learn to be led by Him.

I am including a quote of something Moses spoke to Israel centuries ago because I think the Spirit of Christ that spoke through him looked forward in time to us who were to receive the Holy Spirit and spoke these words of encouragement.

> *Deut 30:10-14 … if you turn to the LORD your God with all your heart and soul.*
>
> *"For this commandment which I command you today is not too difficult for you, nor is it out of reach. "It is not in heaven, that you should say, 'Who will go up to heaven for us to get it for us and*

> ***make us hear it, that we may observe it?' "Nor is it beyond the sea, that you should say, 'Who will cross the sea for us to get it for us and make us hear it, that we may observe it?' "But the word is very near you, in your mouth and in your heart, that you may observe it.***

It seems to me that for most of my years as a Christian, I have approached my walk as if somehow God was going to magically fix me if I would just do "Christian things." I let myself walk led by the flesh while telling myself He was changing me because I was doing those "Christian things." I didn't or maybe couldn't look at my heart honestly to see how hard I was toward Him. I look back now and it almost seems like I was believing an odd superstition that a child might be taken in by; living my life with a heart that was hard and obstinate toward His leading and telling myself that I was becoming a better Christian day by day because I was doing more of my little Christian sacrifices. How foolish it seems to me now that I have begun to understand that what He really wants from me is to follow the ways of Christ spoken to my heart and mind and if I seek to know His way with all my heart and then follow it, this is what will produce ***"the hidden person of the heart, with the imperishable quality of a gentle and quiet spirit"***

At the beginning of this chapter, I shared about how, in my heart, the doing of Christian things unwittingly became a substitute for what should have been my walk with the Lord. But I want to make it clear that while I am saying that just the doing of these things is of little value and that the doing of them on their own is not what is pleasing to God, I am convinced that if our hearts are set on following Jesus by the leading and training of His Spirit, and we do these same Christian things, not because we think in themselves they are pleasing to Him, but if we do them to help focus our hearts on following Him, if we pray to Him to lead us and teach us, if we study His Word to truly learn how to follow Him. If the motives behind the Christian things we do are to keep us in that special secret place of fellowship surrendered to the leading of His Spirit, then all these same little Christian sacrifices become disciplines with immeasurable benefits.

I hope if you see any of this same twisted understanding in the approach of your own walk that I discovered in mine, that you will join me today in putting this sort of useless and dead "works approach" behind us and together we will press forward in faith to walk in a new way led by the Spirit of Christ from within our very hearts.

Chapter 8

FINDING THE ENTRANCE TO A SPECIAL PLACE OF FELLOWSHIP WITH JESUS

Intellectually it may appear that these truths we're going through are just about a choice we make or don't make. The thinking that "You have your walk as I have mine" can seem like a good enough reason to not worry too much about trying to understand the different truths I've been sharing about here. But what makes it so much more than that is what happens when one actually steps out in a surrendered faith to follow the leading of the Spirit from within. I would describe what happened for me as something special and amazing. It has taken me to a level of faith and a sense of fellowship with the Lord that I didn't understand could even exist from any of the studies I had done. It makes me want to shout to all believers, **"You have to find this; you need to find this; do anything you can to find this."**

I think Jesus made references about this "something special" that could happen for believers in the following verses from John.

> ***John 14:21-23 "He who has My commandments and keeps them is the one who loves Me; and he who loves Me will be loved by My Father, and I will love him and will disclose Myself to him." Judas (not Iscariot) *said to Him, "LORD, what then has happened that You are going to disclose Yourself to us and not to the world?" Jesus answered and said to him, "If anyone loves Me, he will keep My word; and My Father will love him, and We will come to him and make Our abode with him.***

There are two promises in these verses that I feel like have happened for me in a special way since I started this new way of walking with Jesus. I want to take a little time and share my thoughts on them with you. ***"I will love him and will disclose Myself to him"*** and ***"We will come to him and make Our abode with him."*** Although Jesus doesn't explain them in detail, they are what I would consider conditional promises. To receive them we must first be one who has His commandment, which I am convinced is the situation existing with everyone who has ever believed in Jesus. If His commandments come from His Spirit within us, then if we "have His Spirit," we will have His commandments. The second part of this conditional promise is we must also be one who keeps His commandments or word, thus proving we love Him. For years I told myself this all was somehow related to believing in Jesus for my salvation, but now, when I look a little deeper at fitting it together with the conditional points of the promises here, I see there is something more for us to try to understand. Consider this thought with me. Under the new covenant, God promises to speak His commandments directly to our hearts and our minds. Doesn't this make all believers the ones who have, ***"My commandments"*** or ***"My word",*** and couldn't it be that the believers who prove they love Jesus by following His word or commandments that come from His Spirit within their hearts, find themselves in a very special place of fellowship that the believers who fight against following this leading never quite find? The one, because of the sincerity of their faith and the way their heart surrenders to the leading of His Spirit, seeks after and follows Him with everything that is within them. They find themselves entering that special place of fellowship where Jesus discloses Himself to them in a way that all the intellectual learning can never find. The other, because of a lack of faith and a heart that hardens itself to the leading from the Spirit, misses out on something special that could have been theirs. They fail to receive fully all that could have been theirs based on these promises.

It is my testimony that I became a believer, but because of my ignorance and the hardness of my heart (that I couldn't see), I failed to understand how to be led by the very Spirit of Christ that was within me. I didn't even know that His word was being spoken to my heart, so failing to keep it or to be lead by it was almost automatic for me. I can look back now and see that I had His guidance available enough within my heart to have walked led by it. However, because of what I considered acceptable behavior, what I let pass for love, and what I let pass as a walk of faith, I was one of the ones who didn't keep His word. I didn't walk set apart being trained and guided by His love, instead I walked ignorant and deceived all the while considering myself to be a very sincere believer. It is sad for me to think about how long this period of my walk lasted. In my ignorance and pride, I walked deceiving myself for close to thirty years. Then, almost by accident, I found a more honest place in my heart with a more sincere faith. I decided to try to walk focused on what would be pleasing to the Lord and not myself. Everything changed for me. The scriptures started to become alive in a way they never had in all my years of studying. Everything about my relationship to the world began to change. From that time to now, following after the leading of His Spirit has been the essence of my walk.

Since that time I have tried to practice whatever disciplines I considered necessary to protect this special place of fellowship I have found. I know how easy it is for me to be pulled back into my old ways of walking; get a little too carried away by all the important things I have to do; care a little too much about money or any of my other material possessions; let myself go undisciplined with the lust of my eyes; find myself caught up in protecting my pride; focusing on and embracing the selfishness of my heart. I have come to the realization that if I choose to embrace the leading of my flesh over the leading of His Spirit in any area of my life, my faith runs the risk of being shipwrecked in a heartbeat and that precious place of fellowship will seem lost and distance.

My faith is not perfected by how much I know, how much I study or how much I do any other Christian thing. It is perfected by how I walk it out throughout my life led by His Spirit and this is always affected by the state of my heart before Him. I think I understand now why faith without works is useless. It is because it will never take us to that special place of fellowship that could be ours if it isn't sincere enough to care about and do what His Spirit directs us to do. What kind of faith is it that would hear His way spoken directly to our heart or our mind and say to itself, "No, I'm not doing it your way Lord?" But isn't this what we do whenever we walk led by our own ways instead of His Spirit?

My testimony from the beginning of this writing has been about my coming to the realization that this leading from Christ, since I became a believer, was always available to me. It was always being spoken to my heart. I was just too blind to see it because of a hard heart that walked deceived by sin and led by my flesh instead of His Spirit. I had His commandments, but because I didn't really love Him the way I should have, I didn't keep them and because I didn't keep them, I didn't ever receive these two special promises. We may obtain to what one might consider almost perfect theology, but it is the one who "keeps His commandments" or walks "led by His word," spoken by the Spirit of Christ within their hearts, who receives these blessings.

If we truly want to find **"the pearl of great price,"** it is this walk of obedience led by His Spirit, coupled with a surrendered heart that will purchase it for us. If we truly want to enter His kingdom, I think we step across the threshold of the entrance of His kingdom and find ourselves in a special place when we let our faith be perfected by the way we walk.

> ***"...for as long as you practice these things, you will never stumble; 2 Pet 1:11 for in this way the entrance into the eternal kingdom of our LORD and Savior Jesus Christ will be abundantly supplied to you.***

I want to try and say this as clearly as I can. I know there is a place we can enter, a state of fellowship we can attain. Call it, "His kingdom"; call it, "The promised land"; call it, "Those who have once been enlightened and have tasted of the heavenly gift"; call it, "Knowing the way of righteousness"; call it, "Becoming partakers of Christ"; call it, "A heart after God"; call it, "Practicing His presence." Whatever we call it, this "place" was purchased for us by the blood of Christ and it is only available to believers. No one else has a right to it. It is our inheritance. It belongs to us and us alone. The world cannot get to this "place." But we must understand that the entrance to this special place of fellowship is not automatic just because we have believed. It is a fruit that happens as the result of how we walk out a sincere faith. A faith that is so sincere that our very lives are changed by that faith as we walk in obedience to it through His Spirit He has made to dwell within us; A surrendering to being led by His anointing in how to walk in a way that is truly pleasing to God, a walk of genuine love both to Jesus and to those in the world around us.

If we can understand how to walk in this genuine love, "Jesus' love," guided and trained by His Spirit within us; if we can get our hearts to a place where they are broken of their own way and set with the intent of a pure motive to please our Lord; if we can grow and perfect our faith to the point where it is sincere enough to trust and follow His way, we will find ourselves in this special place of fellowship with our Lord; If we will walk in this love led by Him in such a way that we always keep a good conscience, we will stay in that place of fellowship all our days. I believe that understanding and finding this special "place of faith" is the goal of all our learning.

> *1 Tim 1:5 But the goal of our instruction is love from a pure heart and a good conscience and a sincere faith.*

It is my personal testimony that this "place of faith" exists and I have found the entrance to it myself. As special as it is to me to walk in an intimate fellowship with the Lord, I know that my 'residence is maintained', so to speak, by having a faith genuine enough to walk by the truths it believes, by abiding in Him. If I love Him I will keep His commandment, and His commandment is about how to walk in love by laying down my own life to show that love. His commandment is about walking in love and the guiding of His Spirit is about teaching us how to do this His way.

> *John 15:12-14 "This is My commandment, that you love one another, just as I have loved you. "Greater love has no one than this, that one lay down his life for his friends. "You are My friends if you do what I command you."*

I have come to realize that no amount of doing Christian things will automatically take one to this "place of faith." No matter how much you read and study your Bible, this alone does not provide the entrance. There are those who give themselves to serve the Lord with all their lives and some with little or no compensation, but even this does not provide the entrance. There isn't any amount of sacrifice or service that on its own will get us into this "place of fellowship" with our Lord. It is a "place" that is attained through faith, and works on their own are of little value to help us get there. Yet, the entrance to this place is just as available to the new believer as it is to the pastor of the mega-church, or the life-time missionary because this place is based on how our heart is before our Lord. I want to make it clear that it is not how we see ourselves or how we judge ourselves that matters. God sees right through to the motives and intents behind everything we do and every thought we have. This "place" is a gift given as the result of a sincere faith. It is a grace that comes by faith and not works.

We can wander for years trying to please God by how good we think we are because of all the great Christian things we do, but aren't we trying to attain to our own righteousness as if it were by works just as Israel did? We will never attain to any kind of righteousness by our works. We need to find that righteousness that comes by faith.

> *Rom 9:30–9:33 What shall we say then? That Gentiles, who did not pursue righteousness, attained righteousness, even the righteousness which is by faith; but Israel, pursuing a law of righteousness, did not arrive at {that} law. Why? Because {they did} not {pursue it} by faith, but*

> ***as though {it were} by works. They stumbled over the stumbling stone, just as it is written, "BEHOLD, I LAY IN ZION A STONE OF STUMBLING AND A ROCK OF OFFENSE, AND HE WHO BELIEVES IN HIM WILL NOT BE DISAPPOINTED."***

I am aware that I am being bold in the claim that I make saying I see a way we must go. I am presenting truths about a gift that is available to all believers, but any of us can deem ourselves unworthy of this gift by hardening our hearts to His voice. We miss His very Word within us while chasing after the ways of our flesh and the ways of this world. Like Israel, even though we are the chosen people of God, we can end up wandering in a dry place with a hard heart, unable to enter into His promises because of a lack of faith and unbelief. He allowed this to happen to Israel as an example to show us that it is not enough to please Him, just because we are His chosen. They were His chosen just as we are. Nevertheless, He was not pleased with how their hearts were toward Him. He wants us to have hearts that care about following the leading of the Spirit of His Son that He has made to dwell within us. There is an entrance for us as believers, to a special place of fellowship, and I am certain that if we can embrace this eighth truth with all our hearts, it will provide that entrance for us. As simply and as clearly as I can put it, **"We need to act on His guidance, not just know it. Learning His truths is of little value if we don't apply them through faith into how we walk in love."**

My hope is that, right now, in reading this, you will be challenged to look carefully at your own heart and your own walk with the Lord. If you see ways where you could walk in love differently, with a more genuine love, if your motives were set only on trying to respond to people in a way that was pleasing to God, then I hope you will follow that leading with all your heart as if it were coming from His Spirit within you. If you see your heart set on things not pleasing to Him, I hope you will step out in faith and set your heart on things that will please Him knowing that it is His Spirit that gives us a heart to see through our own ways. It is my experience that as I have stepped out in faith to follow the way I knew would really be pleasing to Him, my faith and confidence that it is His guidance leading me to understand how to walk pleasing to Him increases. I believe that as we intentionally engage and embrace our faith in the way we walk, it grows. We go from faith to faith perfecting our faith by the way we walk in faith. After awhile, I believe you too will find this kind of faith and it will lead to a truly special place of fellowship with Jesus, our Lord. His promise is to all of us, that He will reward those who seek Him and that He will let those who seek Him with all their hearts find Him.

I am including the following verses from the book of Hebrews because of how they help reinforce my understanding of this walk; how important it is for us to become partakers of Christ today; to enter a rest reserved for those who, by faith, believe in His word. Today as you read through and consider these verses, I hope it will touch your heart with a renewed understanding of what it means to partake of Christ and enter that rest He has for us.

Heb 3:6 - 4-13 but Christ {was faithful} as a Son over His house--whose house we are, if we hold fast our confidence and the boast of our hope firm until the end.

Therefore, just as the Holy Spirit says, "TODAY IF YOU HEAR HIS VOICE, DO NOT HARDEN YOUR HEARTS AS WHEN THEY PROVOKED ME, AS IN THE DAY OF TRIAL IN THE WILDERNESS, WHERE YOUR FATHERS TRIED {Me} BY TESTING {Me,} AND SAW MY WORKS FOR FORTY YEARS. "THEREFORE I WAS ANGRY WITH THIS GENERATION, AND SAID, 'THEY ALWAYS GO ASTRAY IN THEIR HEART, AND THEY DID NOT KNOW MY WAYS'; AS I SWORE IN MY WRATH, 'THEY SHALL NOT ENTER MY REST.'" Take care, brethren, that there not be in any one of you an evil, unbelieving heart that falls away from the living God. But encourage one another day after day, as long as it is {still} called "Today," so that none of you will be hardened by the deceitfulness of sin. For we have become partakers of Christ, if we hold fast the beginning of our assurance firm until the end, while it is said, "TODAY IF YOU HEAR HIS VOICE, DO NOT HARDEN YOUR HEARTS, AS WHEN THEY PROVOKED ME." For who provoked {Him} when they had heard? Indeed, did not all those who came out of Egypt {led} by Moses? And with whom was He angry for forty years? Was it not with those who sinned, whose bodies fell in the wilderness? And to whom did He swear that they would not enter His rest, but to those who were disobedient? {So} we see that they were not able to enter because of unbelief. Therefore, let us fear if, while a promise remains of entering His rest, any one of you may seem to have come short of it. For indeed we have had good news preached to us, just as they also; but the word they heard did not profit them, because it was not united by faith in those who heard. For we who have believed enter that rest, just as He has said, "AS I SWORE IN MY WRATH, THEY SHALL NOT ENTER MY REST," although His works were finished from the foundation of the world. For He has said somewhere concerning the seventh {day:} "AND GOD RESTED ON THE SEVENTH DAY FROM ALL HIS WORKS"; and again in this {passage,} "THEY SHALL NOT ENTER MY REST." Therefore, since it remains for some to enter it, and those who formerly had good news preached to them failed to enter because of disobedience, He again fixes a certain day, "Today," saying through David after so long a time just as has been said before, "TODAY IF YOU HEAR HIS VOICE, DO NOT HARDEN YOUR HEARTS." For if Joshua had given them rest, He would not have spoken of another day after that. So there remains a Sabbath rest for the people of God. For the one who has entered His rest has himself also rested from his works, as God did from His. Therefore let us be diligent to enter that rest, so that no one will fall, through {following} the same example of disobedience. For the word of God is living and active and sharper than any two-edged sword, and piercing as far as the division of soul and spirit, of both joints and marrow, and able to judge the thoughts and intentions of the heart. And there is no creature hidden from His sight, but all things are open and laid bare to the eyes of Him with whom we have to do.

Chapter 9

UNDERSTANDING A WALK OF FAITH

Ninth on the list is the truth that, **"We can only produce fruit if we walk a life led by His Spirit."** As I attempt to explain this, I want to start by going through what I see as the difference between faith and works. The following is a verse in Hebrew's that makes a reference to an idea that should be at the core of our understanding of how to walk out our lives pleasing to God: ***"Heb 6:1: ... not laying again a foundation of repentance from dead works and of faith toward God".*** "Not laying again" should tell us this was understood by the writer to be an essential concept to be grasped at the beginning of any believer's walk. The idea of "repentance from dead works" is an interesting concept to delve in to. Here is what I have come to understand as the correct way of looking at my works, both works of faith, and works that are not of faith and this idea of dead works we need to repent from practicing. As I see it, if a correct understanding of what "dead works" means should be embraced as an elementary and foundational truth which belongs at the core of every believer's walk, then we should all carefully look at this truth and make sure we have a clear understanding of how works are to play into our walks. I believe the answers lie in learning to discern the real difference between deeds of faith and deeds of works.

It has become clear to me that the difference between works done, as the result of faith, and works that are dead, is not in the type of work or deed done, but is in the motive in our heart as we do the work. The difference in the motive behind why we do our works is important because here is where our walks are either led by our flesh or by the Holy Spirit. If we think, even as a believer, that we can decide on our own how to do good and be good by our own leading (our own reasoning), thinking we are pleasing God by our good deeds and by how good we think we are living our lives; if we see ourselves as living a righteous life because of those choices, then our deeds are being motivated by thinking that we are pleasing God by our good works. But if we look at the righteousness of God's ways and say to ourselves, "Real righteousness is God's righteousness and it is so far removed from what we can do directed by our own reasoning" and if we can understand that our "flesh led" personal motives for doing our good deeds contaminate the deeds in such a way that they will never impress God (even though they might seem to impress the people around us), then we will have begun to see through our own self righteous ways. On the other hand, if we begin to do what we know we should because we understand it is what Jesus wants us to do, what He is directing us to do and if we understand, He alone, knows how to correctly decide what is really good and if we do it because we trust His way for us, then we are walking by faith and the deeds or the works are founded in faith not works. One way is us trying to be righteous on our own and the other is trusting and resting in the righteousness of God by faith. Here is a quote from Romans along this line. In it, we see Israel failing to attain righteousness because they are unable to discern how to pursue righteousness by faith. (***Rom 9:31-32 but Israel, pursuing a law of righteousness, did not arrive at {that} law. Why? Because {they did} not {pursue it} by faith, but as though {it were} by works. They stumbled over the stumbling stone,)***

So if we will quietly listen to His word that He has implanted in our hearts and follow its leading in place of our own, His way for us will be perfect, righteous and Holy and the motives for doing it His way, His deeds He has planned for us, are grounded in faith not works. He is pleased because we trusted in Him, because we followed Him, because we acknowledged Him and we listened to the word of Christ planted within our hearts through His Spirit. This way of walking, led by Jesus, is a true and sincere walk of faith.

To help keep our understanding correct about our own works, we have to begin to realize how far removed our ways are from God's ways and start comprehending that true righteousness is in His hands and His hands alone. We can do nothing good on our own. I think if we can attain to a more correct understanding of God's righteousness, it will help to keep us from stumbling over the stumbling block of trying to please God by works instead of faith. If there is anywhere in our walk, as believers, where we need eye salve from Jesus to help us see and understand our true condition, it has to be here. The thinking that we are somehow pleasing to God by our works, when they are not done as a result of faith, is convoluted, twisted and I believe even a bit insulting to God. If we can learn to grasp the concept in our thinking, that if we believe our works are pleasing because of how good they are, then this is actually equal to drawing a comparison between our goodness and what the true righteousness of God is like. While it is a true statement, "*...faith without works is dead." (James 2:26)*, it is just as true a statement, "that works without faith are useless and dead works as well." Remember, where it says in ***Heb 11:6 "And without faith it is impossible to please {Him,} ..."*** Behind this truth lies a reference to someone thinking that God can be pleased by just the kind of works they might do without any connection to faith.

I think most of us as believers have probably lived our lives with the concept that we "do good" as we go about our daily tasks unless we happen to sin. We further develop this thinking, that as Christians, we learn to sin less and less and in time it becomes easier to live a more righteous life that is closer to perfect by our works. I believe we are deceiving ourselves when we embrace this kind of reasoning. Even as believers, we can blindly carry out the desires of our flesh, deed after deed and work after work as that desire lies hidden in the motives behind our deeds and works. We need to wake up to the truth that the only way we can keep from carrying out the desires of the flesh is when we are led by His Spirit. On our own, "there is none who do good not even one, for all of us fall short of the glory of God," by our own works. Even the best righteousness we can accomplish is like filthy rags when we compare it to His. We need to understand that our reasons and motives for doing our good works, if we are not led by His Spirit, are always contaminated by the influences of our flesh and as a result are not really grounded in faith at all.

It might seem like I am splitting hairs with this difference between works of faith and works motivated by a self righteous thinking. But His Word, planted within us, is sharp enough to discern this difference. I am sad to say this, but I think most often the message coming from our teachers does not correctly define the difference and we, the body of believers, receive a maligned message and therefore struggle to understand how to walk pleasing before our God. We then suffer the effects of a corrupted walk. Deceived, because we have so much trouble seeing the difference between these two, we fail to enter the real rest He has for us. But the opportunity to fix this problem, to change our lives and enter the rest He has for us is near to us. Right now it can happen for any believer. We can lay a foundation of repentance toward dead works in our very hearts. This word He has implanted, this anointing He has given us, it is able to guide us into all truth. It is able to set us free from the bondage of a works system and lead us in how to walk by true faith. Only by His Spirit can we truly ever be set free to live a life pleasing to God by faith.

I know we tell ourselves that we have believed in Jesus therefore our walks as believers are by faith. But if you look closely at what James says, ***(James 2:19 You believe that God is one. You do well; the demons also believe, and shudder.)*** it almost seems like he mocks the thought of a faith that is so weak that it tries to rest in an unchanged life by telling itself, "I believe in God" or our current version of, "I believe in Jesus." If you read close in the gospels, you will notice that even the demons always seemed to know who Jesus was and they shuddered at what that meant for them. But are we willing to recognize that if our faith doesn't show up in the core of our hearts, in how we live our lives in obedience to the word of Christ, then we need to be asking ourselves what kind of faith this is?

If any of us wants to know where we should start if we want to be led by the Spirit of Christ within our hearts, I think the first thing we should try to do is to learn to ask ourselves this question. **"What would the love of Christ look like for me if I were to respond the way He would have me respond in this interaction with this person; in this thought of my heart; in this testing and trial I'm dealing with right now?"** If we can find a place in our hearts where we really want to know the answer to this question, because we truly want to guide our lives by that answer, I believe the Spirit will put the answer directly into our hearts and our minds and if we will choose to be led by that answer, we will have entered a sanctified walk. If we will do this over and over throughout the day as we pay attention to the thoughts of our hearts and the things that are happening to us and around us, watching for how to understand His way to walk in love over our way, in time our receptiveness to understanding the leading of His Spirit will grow. If we will also be receptive to taking correction from the Spirit (seeing our faults), God will begin a process of exposing ways about us that we cannot see on our own and that are hurtful to our walk and displeasing to Him. (For example: Selfishness, pride, anxious ways, lust, greed, malice and all the other deeds of the flesh we are so blindly motivated by when we are not led by His Spirit).

If we are going to be sincere, I think this kind of walk needs to be pervasive throughout our entire lives and our entire hearts minute by minute, hour by hour, and day by day. I think it should be how we deal with those we love, (friends and family), and it should also be how we deal with those who are difficult for us. It should be how we deal with co-workers, employers, employees, and neighbors and it should even affect our attitude as to how we conduct ourselves in any and all business or financial matters. If our walk with Him is going to be real, we can't shut out any part of our lives from His direction. As we go throughout the day, we should listen to the conversations that go on in our thinking and we should want His leading for their direction. Finding a way to be led by the Spirit within us in how to walk every thought of our heart pleasing before The Father is the real goal. But we have to care enough about being led by Jesus to seek His way or we will do this our own way. We have to care enough about wanting to please Jesus to pay attention to how we walk out our lives or we will walk out our lives to please ourselves.

The faith part of this exercise is believing that God can and will lead us in knowing His way. The sincerity of heart, needed for this to work, cannot be faked. A sincere heart before an all knowing God is so intensely personal that it can only exist in a one-on-one relationship with Him and no one, but Jesus Himself, can be part of that with us. The simplicity of this walk for me lies in knowing all I have to do is keep a desire to please Him running in my thinking at all times. If my desire is always to please Him, and if by faith I believe that it is possible to know His way, then I will also always have a desire in my heart to know His way and a default setting in my thinking that if I know His way, I will do it. In time, as we walk led by Him, we will grow in our understanding of just how faithful He is to guide us in His way. It really is the everlasting way.

I want to make it clear that I am aware that I don't always discern His way for me correctly with every response. I know that the measure of my maturity as a believer is based on the growth of my faith as I learn to discern His way over mine. The process of being trained by the Spirit of Christ includes Jesus showing me my faults. Victory over my problems seems to lie in my ability to learn to trust that His way is always the best way for me. When He shows me that I have something wrong, anywhere in my walk, it is always because I didn't choose His way for me. This only proves all the more how important it is to become surrendered to finding and following His way. It should be our intention to always care, not just about what we do or say, but to actually want the very motive behind why we do or say things to be pleasing to Him. If our motives are grounded in faith, if our motives are because we believe we know how He would want us to respond in love, and therefore in obedience, we respond how He would have us respond, then we have found a sincere walk of faith.

Now we can walk with a clear conscience about how we follow Him. But in saying this we should understand we are not even really qualified to judge the motives of our own hearts. Because even in this, our hearts are too biased and deceitful to guarantee we can be a good judge. The best we can do is live our life with all our heart (with everything that is within us), trying to follow His way of love for us, with a clear conscience and a sincere faith; led by Jesus; trusting in His power to guide us; to strengthen us; to establish us; to confirm us; and to perfect us. Faith comes down to trusting the (very specific) plan He has for our lives moment by moment all the while understanding how lost we are to get it right without Him. Here is a thought from Paul along this same line of reasoning:

> *1 Cor 4:3-5 ... in fact, I do not even examine myself. For I am conscious of nothing against myself, yet I am not by this acquitted; but the one who examines me is the LORD. Therefore do not go on passing judgment before the time, {but wait} until the LORD comes who will both bring to light the things hidden in the darkness and disclose the motives of {men's} hearts; and then each man's praise will come to him from God.*

If we can find a place in our walks where we become obedient to the teachings of the Spirit of Christ, we will see that the word that He has put within our hearts will bring forth the kind of fruit He desires for each of us. This place where we chase after knowing His way with a heart bent on doing things His way is what I believe is the only true sanctified walk that exist for believers. There is no other way anyone is going to get to know Jesus unless we learn how to walk through this life guided by Him in how to walk in His ways.

The second thing I would say to someone if they wanted to be led by the Spirit of Christ within their heart is to read and study the Bible. If this way of walking I am sharing about touches your heart as truth, then I hope you will go to His word of truth and look for it. As you read, watch for what the Bible teaches about the Holy Spirit; about how important it is to God what goes on in the heart; about love; about fruit coming from obeying the word of Christ. Study what it has to say about the flesh and what it looks and acts like. Look for all that Jesus says about this message I am sharing, in the gospels and especially in John's account. Pay close attention to references to the Word which became flesh and dwelt among us and through His Spirit that now lives within us. I am convinced that if you search for this message about walking led by the Spirit of Christ that is within us, throughout the Bible, with your heart set on changing your life so that you will live it pleasing to Him by what you learn, you will find it is not some hidden mystical message, but that it is a message infused throughout the teachings, not just in the Gospels but that it is a message in the teachings of all the New Testament and that it is also behind all of what happens in the Old Testament too. It is not just a New Testament thought that God wants the hearts of His chosen people, as well as the hearts all men, to seek Him and His ways. It should not be that surprising for us to find out it has always been His desire for the hearts of men from the start. God really is the same yesterday, today and forever.

I know many of us read our Bibles pretty regularly once we become believers, but the difference of what happened for me as I read looking for ways to change my life so that I could truly live it pleasing to Him, is nothing short of amazing. It makes me think of the "magic eye" posters that one can stare at for hours or even days, but then, when you look at them in just the right way, a hidden three dimensional looking image jumps out of the art to be viewed. For thirty years I had studied His Word, but now, I guess, because the motives of my heart had changed, as I read, I saw the message differently than I had ever seen it. This new message jumped off the pages as an amazing, three dimensional, living and active word ready to bring change to my life. I could see it had always been there, but it had been hidden and veiled from my understanding because of the hardness of my heart and my lack of understanding in how to walk by faith. As I searched, with a new purpose in my heart, I found this new living message in every teaching of Jesus' throughout the Gospels, in every letter of the New Testament writings and infused in a bit more of a hidden way, yet supported by all that happened and was taught by the Old Testament writings. I believe that if we will study the Bible, not just to see what it says, but to search for a way to change our life so that we can live it pleasing to God, we will all find this same living three dimensional message jumping off the pages at us.

It seems, as I look back at what happened for me, because of the change in my approach, I proved the principle that faith is perfected by works. It wasn't until I set my heart on finding and implementing His way, the works He had for me to do, into how I lived my life, that His Word began to change my life. Faith was no longer just believing "I was saved" because I had received the gift of salvation by faith. Faith now was receiving life giving direction moment by moment, day by day, growing in trust and finding hope and peace in spite of all the problems that exist around me. My understanding of fruit has changed from thinking it is the deeds themselves, to understanding that fruit really is about the tender changes coming to our hearts as we learn to walk by our faith.

I know that all of us come up with our own way of coping with the various trials of this life. Some of us have studied our own little library of self-help books. Others have engaged in finding guidance from counselors, whether professionals or someone they respect. We look to these sources to try to understand the best way for us to respond to our trials. We work out some combination of our own wisdom and the wisdom we seem to glean from our research and this becomes the understanding we guide our lives by. It appears to our reason that there really is no other way to approach this life. I suppose we can talk to just about anyone we know and they will tell us how they work this out in their lives and they can describe how it all applies for them. I know that this self-help or even the coached-help approach seems to be backed by wisdom, but if we could see ahead to what the results of doing our walk through this life God's way would look like, we would realize that by comparison, this leading our way, by our own wisdom and strength would seem void and useless. Our way possesses no power to help curb the desires of our flesh. In the end, we are still crippled by pride, perhaps even more so. As we learn to set our boundaries, we remain crippled by our selfishness, perhaps even more so. We still carry out the desires of the flesh although with an element of self-control that gives the illusion that it is all good as we walk out our lives. The boastful pride of a self-righteous life that can be hidden in our hearts as a result of how good we think we are at reasoning our way through this life is perhaps the most blinding pride of all.

As Christians, even when we turn the Bible into our own form of a self-help book, the results are not much better for us. But God's way for us, of being personally led by the Holy Spirit, the Spirit of Jesus Christ He has put within us produces a different result; a peace that passes understanding, because it is a peace that exists no matter what turmoil is in our lives or in the world; an incomprehensible joy as we walk moment by moment led by Him that can't be obtained any other way; a genuine love that grows in our hearts for all people, for our loved ones, for our friends, and also for those who are difficult for us; we grow in patience toward all people and all circumstances; the gentle character of our heart increases in kindness, goodness, faithfulness, hope, self-control and true godliness as we grow in faith; we learn to trust not on our own understanding, but we learn to lean on His understanding and follow Him in all His ways; we learn to trust in His faithfulness.

This might hit you as if I'm throwing all kinds of scripture and reasoning at you to convince you of some new doctrine I've come up with, but the truth is I'm sharing a personal witness; a testimony of what has happened for me in my life. I'm sharing that I have tried this both ways, and God's way really does work. No matter how much success man's way might seem to have for us, I assure you, if we can truly find God's way for our life, we will understand how futile man's way really is by comparison. My hope for anyone reading this is that if any of us haven't found this path of a sanctified walk led by the Holy Spirit, that somehow something will click in our thinking and that right now, today, we will embrace Jesus as Lord and King over our life and truly let Him reign from on high in our hearts and that from now on, we will walk this life out His way. Nothing we can gain of value and nothing we can do or accomplish during this life will be able to compare to the value of what will be accomplished by living out our life in love led by Jesus. I pray that He will help us all understand how short our time really is on this earth and that He will help all of us realize how precious and amazing is this opportunity to walk a life led by Him. ***James 4:14*** (we) ***..."You are {just} a vapor that appears for a little while and then vanishes away."*** Let's not waste any of the time we have left.

Chapter 10

LEARNING TO RESPOND TO LIFE IN A WAY THAT PLEASES GOD

How do I really see God as being involved in my personal world? When I started my new way of walking my life with a focus on faith, I began to ponder this question differently. Up to that point, I had only vague conclusions in my thinking as to what God caused to happen or what Satan, the world, or just evil of some kind caused to happen. I hadn't drawn definite conclusions, whether it was because of indifference on my part or just a sense that it was an unknowable concept, I'm not sure, but I didn't have a definite sense of how much or how little I believed God was involved in the things that happened in the world or in my life.

Then I began to think about God's interaction with my world and the world around me from a different angle, not "What does God cause to happen around me?" but rather from the perspective of, "What does God allow to happen?" As I began to examine my life and think about it from this new perspective of, "What does He allow?" I started to find myself feeling quite confident about a series of conclusions I could come to that seemed inarguable. I started thinking about the truths I was experiencing in my life and at the same time looking at the examples of how God can work, if He chooses, that I was seeing in the Bible. Here are a few of the examples that were part of my thinking. I wear glasses to correct my vision, but I see in the Bible that God can heal a man born blind. I am forced to conclude that God has allowed my vision to be impaired, even though He is capable of healing it. My clothes wear out over time and about every six months or so I need to buy new work shoes. But in the Bible I read that Israel wandered for forty years and neither their clothes nor their shoes wore out. I conclude that even though God is able to keep my clothes from wearing out, He chooses to allow them to wear out. In the Bible, I see God control the rain, the sunshine, the hail, the wind and the lightening. I see He is able to control all the weather however He chooses. So, I can conclude that whatever weather I see around me, God has decided to allow it to happen just that way. In the Bible, I see Jesus heal people of all kinds of diseases, but in my world I see that I get sick from time to time. In fact, I can look ahead and know that someday I will deal with a sickness or accident that will lead to my physical death. I know that God could prevent me from getting sick or even from dying and of course He can heal me when I do get sick. So, I must conclude, that because He is able to keep me from getting sick or injured, then if harm comes my way, it is because He has decided to allow this to happen in my life. The real conclusion I am forced to draw as I examine example after example in my world, is that God is able to control anything and everything. I cannot come up with one instance of anything I see, where I would conclude God couldn't have caused it to happen different if He wanted to. So, I am forced to conclude, that anything and everything I see happening around me, is happening just the way it is because God has chosen to allow it to happen just that way.

In Psalm 139, I see King David as exercising a similar line of thought to my approach here. He is considering thoughts he understands as truths about God and then draws his own undisputable conclusions. I want to look at what he shares to further develop some of these thoughts.

> *Ps 139:1-6: "O LORD, You have searched me and known {me.} You know when I sit down and when I rise up; You understand my thought from afar. You scrutinize my path and my lying down, And are intimately acquainted with all my ways. Even before there is a word on my tongue, Behold, O LORD, You know it all. You have enclosed me behind and before, And laid Your hand upon me. {Such} knowledge is too wonderful for me; It is {too} high, I cannot attain to it.*

In the past, when I have read through this psalm, my first thought was, "what a special relationship David had with the Lord," and "how precious he personally seems to be to God." Something about the way David wrote left me concluding that David walked in the confidence that the Lord truly loved him. So when I look at David's thoughts as if they are meditations and conclusions about who God is in his world, I begin to experience a different understanding about what David is saying. I think to myself, wait a second, doesn't God know me and all my ways and where I will go and what I will do next? Doesn't He know all my thoughts before I say anything? Doesn't He know what will roll off my tongue next? As He examines my life, is there anything about me He doesn't know? If I try to wrap my head around how much God knows about my life or how in control of it He could choose to be if He wanted, it's beyond my comprehension. Like David, I must conclude that if I believe God is "all knowing" as David asserts here, then He knows everything that will happen in my world. He knows every move I will make. He knows every thought I will think. He knows all the reasons why I think those thoughts. He knows every word I am going to say even before I say it. From this understanding that "God knows it all" I can conclude that anyone should be able to apply these truths to themselves personally. God knows all of us this completely. David personalized the conclusions he drew from the truth, "God knows all." We have liberty to do the same. We should all realize and understand that the most important relationship anyone can have is with this God who knows all.

If I also understand and believe that God is all Powerful, then I can understand He is able to control anything in my world. He is able to control anything in the entire world. When I think about it carefully, considering God's attributes, I can only conclude that what I see happening is happening because God has chosen to allow it. If the light turns red; if I'm stuck in slow traffic as I'm running late; if I get a flat tire or have car trouble; if I am treated well by those around me; if I am treated poorly; if any harm comes my way. Truly, I have come to the conclusion that everything that is happening in my life is before His eyes and it is within His control as He chooses what He allows to happen. He cares enough about what goes on in my world to scrutinize my path; to know all my ways; to understand my thoughts and my fears. He cares about all the decisions I will make. He knows what I am going through and He knows the desires and the motives of my heart at any given second of time, as I respond to all the tests life brings my way.

> *Ps 139:7-12: Where can I go from Your Spirit? Or where can I flee from Your presence? If I ascend to heaven, You are there; If I make my bed in Sheol, behold, You are there. If I take the wings of the dawn, If I dwell in the remotest part of the sea Even there Your hand will lead me, And Your right hand will lay hold of me. If I say, "Surely the darkness will overwhelm me, And the light around me will be night,"Even the darkness is not dark to You, And the night is as bright as the day. Darkness and light are alike {to You.}*

In the world that David experiences, he knows that no matter where he goes and no matter what goes on around him, God always is there to give him guidance. In our world as believers, we know that the Holy Spirit is available to us in perhaps an even more special way because we are to understand that the very Spirit of God is in resident within our hearts. This is for our benefit so that we can have direct access within our hearts to the guidance that comes from God to enable us to walk pleasing before Him. If we look at what David says here, he seems to experience a special relationship with the Spirit of God similar to the relationship we experience through the Holy Spirit. In this window to his understanding, we see he concludes that God's Spirit is always there to guide him. A conclusion he appears to draw as a result of personally experiencing this truth. Part of my reason for writing all this has been to share about how available and complete this guidance of the Holy Spirit is to lead us in how to respond to all that God allows to happen in our lives in a way that will please Him. I believe that as we learn to recognize this guidance and live our lives in obedience to its ways or commands if you will, I think we also will soon conclude as David does, God is there for us to give to us this guidance; He has not left us alone; He is faithful to be there for us anywhere we go; we can't escape His presence; He is always there within our very hearts.

> ***Ps 139:13-16 For You formed my inward parts; You wove me in my mother's womb. I will give thanks to You, for I am fearfully and wonderfully made; Wonderful are Your works, And my soul knows it very well. My frame was not hidden from You, When I was made in secret, {And} skillfully wrought in the depths of the earth; Your eyes have seen my unformed substance; And in Your book were all written The***

> ***days that were ordained {for me,} When as yet there was not one of them.***

David also walked with the confident understanding that he personally was created by God and that God knew all things about him. Nothing was ever hidden from God; all the days he would be allowed to live were known and decided by God before he was even born. Once again, the truth that "God knows all" brings some personal deductions we can understand as truths and hold as precious in our hearts. I think we can see that God has had a plan for our lives long before we were ever born and that our birth, our creation if you will, was very thought out and intentional.

> ***Ps 139:17-18 How precious also are Your thoughts to me, O God! How vast is the sum of them! If I should count them, they would outnumber the sand. When I awake, I am still with You.***

I see where David gets this thought from. If I stop to think about it, how precious is the concept that God knows and understands all my ways; that His thoughts toward me are really infinite. As infinite as He is God. If I tried to add up all of God's thoughts toward me or towards any of us, it becomes obvious the number of those thoughts would be impossible to imagine.

> ***Ps 139:19-22 O that You would slay the wicked, O God; Depart from me, therefore, men of bloodshed. For they speak against***

> ***You wickedly, And Your enemies take {Your name} in vain. Do I not hate those who hate You, O LORD? And do I not loathe those who rise up against You? I hate them with the utmost hatred; They have become my enemies.***

I have included David's thoughts here about wanting to align with God in how he feels toward the evil and wicked people because I think it is important for any of us to respond toward evil in a way that pleases God. In trying to comprehend the concept that God sees and understands all that is happening in my world, actually in the entire world, I would like to also focus on the concept that God is a loving God. He can allow hard things to happen in my world, but it isn't to be mean to me. It's never for my harm because if God wished me or any of us harm, we would be undone already. God is not without means to accomplish His every wish. After all, He is almighty God. But if we believe that God is a loving God, then we can understand that His love is as infinite as any of His other attributes and His love toward me, toward any of us, is infinite as well.

If the concept that God is a loving God holds up, why would He allow any hard testing to come in anyone's life? I have two main reasons I think about as I look at the testing that happens in my own life. First, if I care to be trained by it, it will teach me about how my heart works and it will perfect my walk of faith as He trains me with that testing. Second, it will provide me with opportunities to choose to respond to His trials and testing in a way that will please Him. I think we can understand that if God is a loving God, then His desire would be for every person on the face of this earth to get it right in the way they respond to anything and everything that He allows to happen in their lives. He would always want anyone to respond in a way that would please Him. I think if we could be honest with ourselves, we would see we do not do this naturally. We can deduct from the fact that He allows us time to change our ways, that in His love and His patience toward us, it is to give us time to change so that we do get it right. But in His infinite wisdom and for His purposes, He has decided to let us choose. If we will believe in His Son, we can have the option to walk according to the guidance that comes from Christ through His Spirit that is within us, or we can choose to walk according to the course of this world under all its influences. If we believe in Jesus, we can be found living our lives to please God, with an obedience that will give glory to Jesus because He is the one who gives the guidance for us to live by in the first place.

You might be thinking, in my neat little world, this all could seem easy enough to believe, but when one looks across the globe to see some alarmingly horrific natural disaster that takes hundreds or even thousands of lives you could ask, "Would I still feel the same if I could put myself in the middle of such chaos?" I don't think we have to look far in this world to see bad or even evil things happening around us even if somehow they never touch us, so we have to wonder, if God is so in control, then why does He allow such things to happen? It seems to me that the only deduction that rings true with my understanding is, God in His infinite wisdom has chosen to allow the world to be this way for a limited time for His purposes. In time, He will change this world and the evil and the suffering from it will pass away. Some day the curse will be removed. I believe we can also rest assured that nothing about any of the evil we witness has escaped God's notice. He will judge it all at a time He has set and in a way He has determined to be just. If Satan is allowed a measure of rule in this world and if He is allowed to reek disaster and devastation during this time, this does not mean he will escape judgment. For me, understanding the completeness of God's judgment is what makes His allowing any evil to exist make sense at all. Jesus one time made the comment about how complete judgment would be by saying, ***"But I tell you that every careless word that people speak, they shall give an accounting for it in the day of judgment". (Matt 12:36)*** Understanding that, I can trust God, in His infinite wisdom, to know how to judge and punish according to what would be right and just in every instance is an incredibly consoling thought. I don't have to fully comprehend His ways to set my trust in them. I think it is a freeing thought to know that God will take care of all judgment for those both near and far from my little world. If someone does me wrong, no matter how small the wrong, God sees it all and His judgments are complete enough to cover it. We may not see evil get its due during our lifetime, but rest assured, vengeance really does belong to God and His judgments and justice will be perfect.

I see that if we can let go of judging by entrusting that to God, it will make a way for us to walk in love to those around us; even those who do us wrong; those who are our enemies; those who might be rude and unjust in how they treat us. We lack the ability to judge correctly anyway because we can't see all the facts. We don't know what is really going on in people's hearts. But God watches the thoughts of every heart and He alone understands our every motive. He really does have the judgment issues in control. Perhaps our learning how to walk in love toward those who seem destined for judgment will win some to trust in Christ as we have and they will escape the error of their ways.

> ***Ps 139:23-24: Search me, O God, and know my heart; Try me and know my anxious thoughts; And see if there be any hurtful way in me, And lead me in the everlasting way.***

I find it interesting that in these verses we see David invite God to "search him and know his heart." As David has previously told us that he understands "God knows all" and by that nature would of course already know his heart. Inviting God to search our hearts seems like a great way of acknowledging and embracing God for who and how He is, but then to further invite God to try or test us for any anxious thoughts, as David does here, could be a little scary if we are not convinced God is a loving God. Why does David do this? I think the underlying reason in this context seems to be that anxious thoughts indicate a lack of trust on David's part in God's plan for Him. David further invites God to see if there is *any* hurtful way in him. He wants God to show him if there is anything in him that he is doing in thought or deed that doesn't please God because David really does want to get it right. It is, however, the very last thought in this psalm that is the most important culmination of every thought it contains. David is asking God to lead him in the everlasting way. I think we can all understand that the everlasting way for David would have been; a way that would please God; a way designed and desired by God for David's life. But doesn't David's asking God to lead him in the everlasting way also show us that David understood he needed God to help him understand how to get it right as he walked out his way through life?

If we want to think that we understand these truths that become so clearly evident and undeniable as we look at what we can know about the attributes and nature of God, then don't we need to walk out our lives moment by moment under the influences that an understanding of them should bring? If we are going to have a true walk of faith, then we must set our hearts on wanting to respond to anything God might choose to allow to happen in our lives, in a way that will please Him; to trust Him that all that happens is part of a plan that He has for our life; a plan to bring our faith to a maturity that will cause our walk to look like that of Jesus'. When His plans for us have had their perfect result, then the fruit our lives will produce will be that our love will look like the love of Christ and all of the world will know we are disciples of Jesus' by that love. But for this to take place, we need to be open and honest before Him about how we walk out every thought of our hearts. How we do this should matter to us because it matters to Him. Let us find that way to be known and led by the Spirit of Jesus Christ that He has caused to dwell within us. Then, like David, we will understand how to please God as we walk out our life led by Jesus in the everlasting way.

I think one of the most important thoughts or conclusions I have come to as I have tried to understand how to get it right in my own walk is that **God is involved and in control of all that happens around us. He is in control of all the testing and trials that take place in our lives** and that I do not have the capacity to understand and choose correctly on my own of how I should respond to His testing in a way that will please Him. I must learn to find and rely on the guidance that comes from His Spirit. This and this alone will please Him. The fruit of being led and trained by that guidance will have its perfect result as Christ is formed in me. It is my hope that you will join me in this same quest to walk moment by moment responding to the trials and testing that God allows with the leading that comes through the Holy Spirit. If we truly desire to please the Father, then if we can learn to do this in obedience to Jesus' guidance, we will finally find the way to fulfill that desire.

Chapter 11

A WALK OF LOVE EMPOWERED FOR VICTORY

As I write this, it has been just over seven years since I had what I refer to as my "epiphany." It was at that time that, for whatever all the reason I might dream up as to why God allowed it to happen, the eyes of my heart were opened a little to see how deceptive and sick my heart really was and as a result it allowed me to see through to areas where I was hard toward what He wanted me to do. I was hard toward hearing His commandments as He spoke them to my heart throughout the day. This had been happening even while I might, in my little quiet time with the Lord every morning, read through the Bible about how He would want me to live my life. As I have talked about in past chapters, my hard and deceptive heart kept this sickness up for years. There was, if you will allow the analogy, a corruption in my operating system. Now, when I got saved, the Lord, through the Holy Spirit, had provided an updated fix that could deal with this corruption, but the catch was, I had to choose to run the update at all times for the fix to be effective. The corruption of my operating system was always present (the tendency to be led by my flesh), but when the update was running (being guided directly by the Holy Spirit), the effects from the corruption of my operating system were not a problem (I didn't carry out the deeds of my flesh). While the update was running (abiding in Him by walking the sanctified walk), I was able to live a life pleasing to God. At all other times, the corruption was having its effect (walking led by my flesh). So why am I sharing this now? After seven years of trying to keep "this fix" running at all times, I have noticed, as I have shared and fellowshipped with other believers, that I don't see much evidence that others seem to know how to run "the fix" correctly to get the desired effect. It seems to me, because of how sick and deceptive our hearts are, most can't see a need to live their lives by running "the fix" (change how we are abiding in Jesus) let alone understand how "the fix" works (there is a way to hear directly from Him in our hearts so that we won't carry out the desires of the flesh).

So here is what I think is wisdom about our hard sick hearts. After trying to keep "the update" running 24/7 since my epiphany, I see that my heart is still just as susceptible to being led by my flesh as it ever was. "The fix" didn't change that. But if I will be led by the Holy Spirit as I should be, I don't carry out the deeds of the flesh (the corrupted operating system I live with has no effect). A little more wisdom about our hard sick hearts, even when we want to live our lives to please God our flesh doesn't want us to look at how sick we are; it doesn't want us to know how hard we are; it doesn't want us to see if we get it wrong. Our flesh does not want us to have to change anything about how we are and our hearts can seem very comfortable and almost as if we enjoy living life being led by our flesh. That really is how deceptive our hearts are. But as believers the Spirit within our hearts will never let us feel a true peace or find a genuine joy if we are being led by our flesh. The Lord has allowed me to see some of the hardness and deceptiveness of my own heart as I have had the opportunity over the last seven years to watch my heart deal with trying to run "the fix" (to put to death the deeds of the flesh by the power of the Holy Spirit). My flesh is at odds with my Spirit and my Spirit is at odds with my flesh. The two of them do not get along.

> *Gal 5:16-17 But I say, walk by the Spirit, and you will not carry out the desire of the flesh. For the flesh sets its desire against the Spirit, and the Spirit against the flesh; for these are in opposition to one another, so that you may not do the things that you please.*
>
> *Rom 8:4-15 so that the requirement of the Law might be fulfilled in us, who do not walk according to the flesh but according to the Spirit. For those who are according to the flesh set their minds on the things of the flesh, but those who are according to the Spirit, the things of the Spirit. For the mind set on the flesh is death, but the mind set on the Spirit is life and peace, because the mind set on the flesh is hostile toward God; for it does not subject itself to the law of God, for it is not*

even able {to do so,} and those who are in the flesh cannot please God.

However, you are not in the flesh but in the Spirit, if indeed the Spirit of God dwells in you. But if anyone does not have the Spirit of Christ, he does not belong to Him. If Christ is in you, though the body is dead because of sin, yet the spirit is alive because of righteousness. But if the Spirit of Him who raised Jesus from the dead dwells in you, He who raised Christ Jesus from the dead will also give life to your mortal bodies through His Spirit who dwells in you.

So then, brethren, we are under obligation, not to the flesh, to live according to the flesh-- for if you are living according to the flesh, you must die; but if by the Spirit you are putting to death the deeds of the body, you will live. For all who are being led by the Spirit of God, these are sons of God. For you have not received a spirit of slavery leading to fear again, but you have received a spirit of adoption as sons by which we cry out, "Abba! Father!"

I am sharing this as clearly as I can in hopes that for some it might click as to the gravity of the problem we are dealing with here. **(Our hearts are, not were, desperately sick.)** If we have any desire to walk pleasing before God, we have to see this about our hearts. If we don't own up to the problem and don't see the need to walk a life led by the Holy Spirit, then how are we ever going to understand what it means to be led by the Spirit of Christ, much less how to be led by Him? If we are in the flesh (and we are if we are not walking led by His Spirit), then doesn't it make sense that we cannot please God by our walk if we don't act upon the guidance that comes from His Spirit? I am not making this up and I am hoping as you have read the verses I just shared that you can see this truth. I'm wondering if any of us are really capable of fully comprehending how messed up we are when we are not walking led by His Spirit?

As I have tried to walk this walk, there has been a growing revelation within me about how messed up my approach to decisions are if I just do what comes natural. I feel like I have barely been able to get a glimpse of my tendencies toward selfishness if I am not careful to consider how Jesus would want me to walk in love. I am growing in my awareness of how much the influences of pride are seated in the background of my heart ready to be the motivation to my response if I react without focusing carefully on what He would want me to do first. I think I am also becoming more honest with myself about how easy it is to desire the things and the pleasures of this world. The realization that my heart can easily be hard toward what Jesus might want me to do and how easy it is for me to deceive myself if I am not careful to see things His way, is both scaring me and encouraging me into being caring, careful and conscious toward His desires about everything I do. In the past, my demise has been how I considered it okay to respond to trials anyway I thought best, but unaware of this hardness that I have toward seeing what would be His way for me to respond. Now I have found something that is precious and real and I don't want to mess this up by being careless, blind or hard toward His ways anywhere in my life.

As I have walked this walk, I have actually been proving to myself that a true sanctified walk really does work; that what Jesus taught really works; that He is always there to guide me how to respond correctly; that it is okay to surrender to His way; that I can actually trust Him to cause everything to work together for my good and that it is always okay to walk in love. You might want to ask, won't people take advantage of me or walk all over me if I try to walk in love this way? The answer is, yes, they probably will (He sort of promised us that they will, they did it to Him), but it will still be alright. Jesus knows exactly what we are going through. He will deal with how other people are. We just need to care about how His plans are guiding us and helping us to love in a way that is pleasing to Him. I can see now that He really does weave anything that can happen to us in such a way that it will always help us grow in faith. As I walk this out, day by day, I feel like I am being trained by the little things I am going through to be able to handle whatever hard things the world might throw at me.

As a result of this walk, I really am excited about life. I can hardly wait to wake up and start each new day. Every day seems filled with the revelation of new discoveries and understandings about how to react to the world around me in a way that I know will please the Lord. As I read the Bible, I am daily in awe at how clear the message Christ brought about how to walk with Him now appears to me. My resolve to walk a life of faith is being reinforced by the revelation brought in teaching after teaching coming from verse after verse. I am now more confident about how to be led by His Spirit because of those teachings. I can almost feel my faith grow moment by moment as I learn how to respond from the Holy Spirit in a way that will be pleasing to God. This intimate relationship of being guided and trained by the Holy Spirit makes me feel like I have found the sweetest sweet spot of fellowship that can possibly exist.

One of the things I am the most excited about is that I have found a Christianity that really works. There is victory over the sin in my life and the leadings of my flesh in a way that I had no idea could be possible. Bad habits and patterns of sin I have walked in my whole life, including my struggles to have victory over them through my early years as a believer, are now seeming to me as if they are almost no temptation or test at all. I want the way I walk my life and the victory over sin He provides to prove my love for Jesus and all He has done for me. I know the difference for me now is because He somehow empowers me to have that victory in a way that didn't seem possible in the past when my walk was really founded in works not faith.

The context of my understanding about this difference is that because I have taken the initiative to obey His commandments (that He is quietly speaking to my heart), by stepping out in faith and trust, He now supplies the power for victory on the basis of that faith. I know that even now, if I were to stop taking the initiative to trust Him and believe that I can live my life by His commands, I would be left being led by my flesh and once again nothing would be different for me. I have to keep walking by faith throughout the day, every day, for this to work as He intended.

I feel like I am living proof that faith is perfected by works. But I understand now that the motivation behind the works needs to be grounded in faith as well or the works will be as useless as ever. I think we need to understand that all the believer has to do is step out in faith and obedience to the Spirit of Christ speaking within their heart about how they should do things and the power to do what the Spirit desires will be theirs. As we do this victory anywhere and everywhere in their lives will be within our grasp because the power to walk as He would have us walk, will come from Him on the basis of our faith and our faith will grow in maturity as it is exercised over and over throughout the day and throughout our walk. As our faith grows, I see now that it becomes more and more natural to walk led by the Holy Spirit instead of our flesh. The simplicity of this gospel and the power it possesses for victory is something I am excited to share with the people I love; with my family, friends, and anyone else who will listen. I am excited for anyone to find these same experiences of victory I have found. I can see that there is no addiction; no sin; no problems in our lives that a walk of true faith won't be able to empower us to have victory over.

As I read in the book of Acts and throughout the New Testament Epistles, I can see that this sanctified way of walking I have found is what the writers were hoping their readers would find and be encouraged to walk in at all times and for all times. The expectation within the early church was that every believer would be guided in this way by Jesus' anointing. This walk wasn't supposed to be reserved for just a few that the Holy Spirit might anoint and the thinking that it was somehow just for the mature Christian to engage in is wrong as well. This walk is for the babes in Christ because maturity comes as a result of the walk itself. I will concede that it's only for the sincere Christians who will set their hearts on following Jesus in order to live a life pleasing to God. But becoming a sincere Christian is a choice that any of us can make at any time. How we choose to live our lives is in our hands. We don't need anyone else to choose this walk first so we can follow them. We don't need one other person on the face of this earth to really understand what the walk is all about. It is enough for us to walk it ourselves because this needs to be about our choosing to please Jesus, not other people. He cares about our heart toward Him and our walk with Him. If we genuinely believe in Jesus enough to walk led by Him, we will be different than we have ever been. He will set us free from our selfishness, from the desires of this world and from our boastful pride to walk in His perfect love and we really will be free. He is truly the author and perfecter of our faith. ***(Heb 12:2 fixing our eyes on Jesus, the author and perfecter of faith, ...)***

I know it's possible for any believer to have fallen short of understanding the simplicity of this sanctified walk the way the Lord intended it and that if they knew what they had wrong, they could take steps to correct it. So, I think if anyone genuinely wants to examine themselves, it is possible to test yourself to see if you are walking in faith correctly. Here are a few thoughts to keep in mind that might assist any of us in that examination if we are really interested in looking at ourselves honestly. These should help us both to look at ourselves to make sure we have our core walk of faith correct, and at the same time help us to look at our walk of faith for blind spots where we may have unintentionally hardened our heart toward the leadings of Christ from within. I know if we will set our hearts on genuinely seeking His truths, the anointing of Christ that we have received will lead us into knowing if we have understood His truths and whether we are walking in them correctly. (*1 John 2:27 As for you, the anointing which you received from Him abides in you, and you have no need for anyone to teach you; but as His anointing teaches you about all things, and is true and is not a lie, and just as it has taught you, you abide in Him.)* Unfortunately, as I have tried almost desperately to emphasize, it is all too easy for us to harden ourselves to seeing how we really are, so for this examination to be helpful, we need to be honest before God and with ourselves and we need to be willing to look at how we really are. We need to be reliant on the Holy Spirit to help us see the truth about ourselves. Let me be clear, I am not focusing on the question, "Have we believed in Jesus for our salvation from hell?" I am trying to share truths with those who have already believed, I want to focus on this question, "Is our walk really a walk of faith that is pleasing to God?"

Here is a verse to give a little scriptural precedence for an examination of this sort.

> *2 Cor. 13:5 Test yourselves {to see} if you are in the faith; examine yourselves! Or do you not recognize this about yourselves, that Jesus Christ is in you--unless indeed you fail the test?*

Paul, in this first verse, exhorts the Corinthians to test and examine themselves, if they are in the faith.

Because of how deceptive our hearts can be, I think we should make every effort to honestly examine our walk. The thought that some of us could fail to be found walking in faith in a way that is pleasing to God is truly a sad thought. (A side note: Paul wants them to keep the thought in mind, "Know this about yourselves that if you have believed in Jesus then Jesus Christ is in you." I think it is important to our walks, as believers, that we recognize the truth that "Jesus Christ is in us." Ultimately this should effect how we think, act and live out our lives.)

Here is a verse from 1st John that will help us know how to examine ourselves.

> ***1 John 2:3-6 By this we know that we have come to know Him, if we keep His commandments. The one who says, "I have come to know Him," and does not keep His commandments, is a liar, and the truth is not in him; but whoever keeps His word, in him the love of God has truly been perfected. By this we know that we are in Him: the one who says he abides in Him ought himself to walk in the same manner as He walked.***

John asserts here that we can know if we have it right and are abiding in Christ correctly; if we walk in the same manner as He walked; if we keep His commandments; if we keep His word. So the way to know if we are truly walking out our faith as we should is to look at the way we walk out our daily lives. This will help us see how we abide in Him through our sanctified walk. Does our walk exhibit the perfected love of Jesus coming through us? Do we love those we deal with throughout the day as Jesus would? Do we hear through the Holy Spirit; His word; His way and then do we do it? If we look at ourselves and we see that we don't pass this test, then we need to stop deceiving ourselves about our love for Jesus because we do not know Him as we could; as we should. Husbands look at how you treat your wives; wives look at how you treat your husbands'; not just how you treat them some of the time, but look closely at every interaction. Do you ever feel it is okay to not walk in love because of how they are; maybe you think sometimes they don't deserve to be treated with love? The truth is, if we look at ourselves and find even one time throughout the day, or for that matter throughout the year, where we have chosen to not respond lovingly, then we have failed to walk in the perfected love of God. If we can choose to fail to walk in love toward our wives, our husbands or anyone the way Jesus would want us to, then we have not come to know Him as we should. If we withhold our love, no matter how justified we feel, we have failed the test. But if we choose to walk in love even when we are treated harshly and unjustly, this finds favor with God. ***("For we have been called for this purpose")***

> ***1 Pet 2:18-21 Servants, be submissive to your masters with all respect, not only to those who are good and gentle, but also to those who are unreasonable. For this {finds} favor, if for the sake of conscience toward God a person bears up under sorrows when suffering unjustly. For what credit is there if, when you sin***

> ***and are harshly treated, you endure it with patience? But if when you do what is right and suffer {for it} you patiently endure it, this {finds} favor with God. For you have been called for this purpose, since Christ also suffered for you, leaving you an example for you to follow in His steps,***

In proposing this examination, I do not want to take over the job of the Holy Spirit and become a guide or a judge as to how anyone should be led as they are trained by the Holy Spirit. That needs to come from the Holy Spirit, but we need to be honest with both God and ourselves about how we are, and we need to lean on Him and acknowledge Him in all our ways to get our walks right. This sanctified walk is about a process where, by God's perfect plan, we are destined to be conformed to the image of Christ as Christ is formed in us. Our actions and motives will be pleasing to Him if we set our hearts on knowing and following Jesus' way that comes to our hearts through the Holy Spirit that lives in us. If we are led by His Spirit and walk in obedience to His way for us, we get it right and don't carry out the desires of our flesh. If we look at ourselves and we see Jesus showing us anywhere where we have fallen short of obeying His leading in the way we have responded, to either the people around us or the things of this world, then we should be affected by our failure, we might feel sad or sorry we have fallen short and we should have a resolve to be more obedient and careful to follow His leading in the future. (As He says, "If we love Him we will keep His commandments.") Any failure, of any magnitude, no matter how small, even once throughout the day, should cause us to feel something is wrong, we might even feel estranged from fellowship with Him and it will leave us with a choice. Are we willing to obey His direction to repair our fellowship with Him or not? If we defend or excuse ourselves, then we are no longer abiding in Him nor walking a sanctified walk as we should. True repentance, seems to me, is when we can go to a place of honesty and surrender in our hearts; where we feel bad about our not getting something right; where we can truly say to Jesus we don't ever want to get it wrong again and where we want to know what needs to happen to repair our failure.

If we examine ourselves and see evidence of being led by our flesh, we can know that it is because of His Spirit that we see it. This is part of His plan in training us in how to always be led by His Spirit so we won't carry out the leadings from our own flesh. I don't believe there is any condemnation for us as we are being trained according to His plan if He shows us any of the workings of our flesh. But if we harden ourselves to the direction of His correction, no matter how small, then we are no longer abiding in Him and walking a sanctified walk as we should. I think we should have the understanding that we need to be especially careful to keep a clear conscience regarding what He shows us about our failures, even regarding small things if we don't want to undermine the growth of our faith. We need to understand that the leadings of our flesh are ever present in us and that it is our natural default to be guided and influenced by these leadings in the choices we make, and unless we are walking the sanctified walk correctly, by seeking to be led by His Spirit, we will carry out the desires of the leadings of our flesh. It's just what we will do. We can't help it.

If we want to know His way for us in how to respond to the things that come our way, I believe a good way to do this is to simply look within our hearts as we ask ourselves, "What would the love of Jesus look like here;" or "did we respond in love" like Jesus would want us to? His real commandment to us is to love one another and we know that a genuine love will always be the perfect fulfillment of what He desires from us. We should know that He is always available to guide us in how to walk in His kind of love and His guidance will always be perfect. We can trust, by faith, that He really will speak His ways to our hearts and our minds. We don't need to doubt. But if we come upon some troubling area of question, we can always go to Him and ask for help to know how we should respond to any test this life brings our way. ***(James 1:5 But if any of you lacks wisdom, let him ask of God, who gives to all generously and without reproach, and it will be given to him.)***

Now, if we want to examine ourselves as we go throughout the day, another good question to ask ourselves might be, "Are we seeking His guidance or are we really guiding ourselves by just doing what we think is best?" His guidance will be able to see through to the motive behind how we make our decisions. This is something we are not capable of doing without His help. It is not necessarily that we will do things all that different as to the deeds themselves under His guidance, often it has more to do with the reason behind why we do them. An example might be, if we are nice to people so they or others will notice how we are being good toward them, (maybe to get them to like us or think well of us), is different than if we are trying to walk in love toward them out of a desire to please the Lord. Jesus cautioned us that we should be aware of our motives as to why we are being good by saying it this way, ***"Beware of practicing your righteousness before men to be noticed by them; otherwise you have no reward with your Father who is in heaven.*** *(Matt 6:1)* There is no reward for us because we aren't trying to please God, but man. But how different is the thought that, "I can't see righteousness correctly without His guidance, so I will do what He says and trust Him to lead me how to walk in love correctly in a way that will be pleasing to the Father," rather than our trying to do what we consider good so that others around us will notice our deeds and think well of us.

Another good question we can be asking ourselves is, "Do we see obvious signs of the flesh in the way we act or react to things?" Here is a bit of a list of what the deeds of the flesh might look like from the letter to the Galatians: ***(Gal 5:19-21 Now the deeds of the flesh are evident, which are: immorality, impurity, sensuality, idolatry, sorcery, enmities, strife, jealousy, outbursts of anger, disputes, dissensions, factions, envying, drunkenness, carousing, and things like these,)*** This of course is not a complete list of all the flesh like deeds we deal with, as Paul says, ***"and things like these"*** so we can add to it any other ***"things like these"*** we might come up with from our own observations as well as ***"things like these"*** we might discover as we study the Scriptures. But the real place we should be careful to watch for ***"things like these"*** is in our own lives. Do we see anything that's on the list or even something like what's on the list going on in our lives or maybe just in the thinking within our hearts? Now if we look at how we are and we do see evidence of any of these in the way we react to things around us, we can pretty much rest assured that we are being led by our flesh.

We should be looking at the anger that goes on in our hearts; the envy; the desire; the lust; the jealousy; the disputes we deal with; and we should be looking at how we handle sensuality. If we look honestly at the thoughts of our hearts and we see evidence of any of these, we should be concerned about how we deal with that reality. If we see we are carrying out any of the deeds of the flesh as we look at ourselves, then we are being led by our flesh. We should want to know this. We need to know this because it is not okay to be led by our flesh. If we tell ourselves we are followers of Christ and yet walk our lives led by our flesh we are deceiving ourselves. The truth is that if we see these things, we are not the followers of Christ as we could be.

But if we are being trained by the Holy Spirit, and the things happening to us throughout the day expose the influences of the flesh while we are desiring to be led by Him, this can help us see how we are and we can choose to stop the travel in that direction by the power of His Spirit. This is when we are putting to death the deeds of the flesh as we should; this is His desire for us; this is what brings glory to Christ and this is a sanctified walk as it should be. He has a plan for us and He is working in our lives to perfect us. In time, His plan will bring about the fruit He desires. That will be the evidence of the changes happening, as the tendency to be led by our flesh, which produces these types of deeds, is purged out of our lives by His power and as our faith grows, we will see that it becomes more and more natural to walk led by the Holy Spirit instead of our flesh. But if we exhibit evidence of any of these deeds, whether we take the effort to notice them or not, we are walking led by our flesh. Let's not fool ourselves. If we are making justifying excuses in our hearts as to why we don't need to do something about them, then we are not walking in fellowship with Him in a sanctified life as we should. We are actually exhibiting evidence of being obstinate, stiff necked and hard hearted toward His leading. If we are believers and are somehow thinking we don't have this tendency and we don't need to watch for or worry about carrying out the deeds of our flesh, I think we have missed the whole point, the core purpose of the sanctified walk.

If we really love Jesus, then we need to care about the sin that goes on in our hearts and in our lives. We need to care enough to want Him to help us see it and we need to care enough to surrender to His plan and believe in His power to set us free from sin. Today, as we look at how we walk out our lives, if we see any place where Jesus is speaking to our hearts about how to walk in love (the way He would want us to) let's not harden our hearts, but rather become obedient and surrender our hearts to be guided by His perfect plan. Let's give up on our useless and dead way of works and enter the rest that can only be found in trusting in His perfect plan. We will find the true power of our Christian walk of faith when we find that brokenness that leads to a complete surrender to seek Jesus' way in how to walk out our lives. Then, all the fullness of the fruit that comes from a sanctified walk will truly be ours. Today, let's make a choice that will change our lives forever by committing our hearts to listen to and obey the quiet whisper which comes into our hearts and our minds from the Spirit of Jesus Christ to lead and empower us in how to walk in His perfect love.

Chapter 12

LIGHTS SHINING IN A DARK PLACE

The twelfth and last truth, from those I listed in the introduction is: **It is entering this walk of obedience to the leading of His Spirit through faith that will truly make us different from all other people.** I know that those of us who have believed in Jesus for our salvation are different from all other people on the face of this earth. We are different because of the gift of the Holy Spirit that was given to us the moment we believed. The Holy Spirit was given to us by God to bring about our redemption from the corruption that is in this world. We are truly a chosen people, (the Israel of God, if you will). It is the miracle of this moment of faith when we set our trust in Jesus that we were sealed in Him with the gift of the Holy Spirit. It is this gift of the Holy Spirit which has made it possible for us to live our lives differently as well. It is by the Spirit that we are enabled to know God's way; it is by the Spirit that we are empowered to walk His ways out in our lives. This is God's perfect plan for us, made possible by the sacrifice of Christ on the cross. He purchased this redemption for us. The cost was paid by the death He died and the blood He shed.

> *Eph 1:13-14 In Him, you also, after listening to the message of truth, the gospel of your salvation--having also believed, you were sealed in Him with the Holy Spirit of promise, who is given as a pledge of our inheritance, with a view to the redemption of {God's own} possession, to the praise of His glory.*

But for us to be different in how we respond to God and eventually in how we appear to the world, we need to enter a walk of obedience through faith, to the leading of His Spirit. This kind of a walk of faith is the only way that we will truly look different from all other people. We will become different because of the fruit that is produced in our lives as a result of this sanctified walk. It will enable and empower us to escape the desires and the lust of our hearts which are responsible for bringing about the corruption of our lives as we walk in this world. It is through the sanctified walk that we begin to share in our inheritance as fellow heirs with Christ. It is by our faith, which we walk in **right now**, during this life we live, that we truly begin to share in His divine nature.

> *2 Pet 1:4 For by these He has granted to us His precious and magnificent promises, so that by them you may become partakers of {the} divine nature, having escaped the corruption that is in the world by lust.*

It is part of our inheritance as believers, that by the power of His promises, we can be enabled to escape the corruption that comes from the lust of our flesh. This is the corruption that has us chasing after the ways of this world. And, we truly can lay aside every encumbrance that would keep us from walking in that power. As I see it, these encumbrances are primarily comprised of all that it will cost us to follow Christ. We need to believe that we really can lay aside the sins which can so easily entangle us. This is what will allow us to run this race of faith the way God intended. Individually, there is something to be done by each of us, in the way we live our lives, **right now, and daily.** This walk isn't just about seeking for the opportunity to share about Jesus with the non-believer, it is just as much, if not more, about walking in love toward God, moment by moment, as we prove that love by listening to the whispering directions from His Son within our hearts; guiding and empowering us in how to walk in love to all those we encounter throughout the day; guiding us and empowering us in how to respond within our hearts to the trials of this world in a way that is pleasing to the Father. This is the everlasting way to walk that truly pleases the Father as we glorify His Son by our obedience to His ways for us. This way of walking by faith, as we experience the power of His promises, is what will overflow our hearts with a desire to share with everyone we encounter about the wonders of the unfathomable love of God that we see and experience in, through, and from Christ Jesus.

> ***Heb 12:1 Therefore, since we have so great a cloud of witnesses surrounding us, let us also lay aside every encumbrance and***

> ***the sin which so easily entangles us, and let us run with endurance the race that is set before us,***

We need to focus on the salvation **that is ours now**; the redemption **that is ours now**; the ability to be free from the power of sin **that is ours now**; the power to escape the corruption of the world **that is ours now**; the sharing of His divine nature **that is ours now**. I think all too often we look at our inheritance as only that which we will receive after we have died and are with Christ. We need to understand **that right now,** we have eternal life because we know Christ. Because we have believed, we will live even if we die. **Right now,** death no longer has power over us. **Right now,** He is our King and we can be His subjects and His every wish can be our command. **Right now,** our sanctified walk will supply the entrance into His kingdom. The true prize we go after, the rewards to come and the riches stored in heaven for us, are all for those of us **who seek Him now. Right now** is our opportunity to bring glory to Christ by the way we live our lives in all the power supplied to us by His victory. **Right now,** Jesus is alive. **Right now,** He sits at the right hand of the throne of God. Somehow, we need to walk in the faith and in the hope of living a life pleasing to God, **now.** If we will truly do this, then we really will look different from the rest of the world. The world will look at us in awe of the love we have for each other and the love that reaches out to them. I know that we need to walk this individually and, of course, the world will see us individually, but the true body of those abiding in Christ is made up of the collection of those who will make Him their king, **right now during this life we are**

living. This is the body of believers that truly looks different from the rest of the world. These are the ones He is not ashamed to call His brethren. These are the ones that can be identified by how different their love looks. If we are believers and are not part of this group, it is probably because of our own stubbornness and hard hearts. It is not because Christ has fallen short of purchasing it for us. **We need to choose His way today. Let's not wait for tomorrow.** If Jesus Christ is in us, we are already different from the rest of the world. **Let's live that difference out now in the way we walk led by Him.**

My prayer for all of us who have Jesus Christ living within, and I include myself in this prayer, is that God will soften our hard hearts and help us see past our hearts deceitfulness so that we will know His way; that He will lead us in a way that will purify the motives of all we do and teach us how to walk honestly, open and pleasing before Him with every thought of our hearts; that He will help us to discern correctly how to walk in love to those we love and give us wisdom to help us avoid being led by our own flesh; that He will give us the courage to act upon all He desires for us and bring growth into our lives today and each day as we walk with Him; that He will help us to see how to carry His love to those around us in a way that will truly be pleasing to Him.

Father, give us hearts to be the light of Jesus Christ shining for the entire world to see. Amen.

ABOUT THE AUTHOR

Don Latimer grew up in a family of ten children. As a young man he became a carpenter by serving an apprenticeship with his father and uncle. Over the years he honed his craft by observation through trial and error as he went on to build boats, remodel and build new homes and eventually transition his work into a focus on decorative finishes using cement plaster as his medium. His journey and walk with Christ happened in a similar way. He watched, listened and read his Bible as he practiced his faith. When he came to a place where his heart was opened to look honestly at himself, his faith and his walk with the Lord then his whole life changed. His heart was ready to receive what Jesus had wanted him to have from the moment he had believed.

Don lives with his wife Michelle in Washington State. They were married in 1971 and again in 2010. They have three children and seven grandchildren.

Printed in the United States
By Bookmasters

Printed in the United States
By Bookmasters